The ONE YEAR® MINI

FOR
Busy Women

Jennifer King

Tyndale House Publishers, Inc.
Carol Stream, Illinois

Visit Tyndale's exciting Web site at www.tyndale.com

TYNDALE and Tyndale's quill logo are registered trademarks of Tyndale House Publishers, Inc.

The One Year is a registered trademark of Tyndale House Publishers, Inc.

The One Year Mini for Busy Women

Designed by Beth Sparkman

Edited by Linda Schlafer

Unless otherwise indicated, all Scripture quotations are taken from the *Holy Bible,* New Living Translation, copyright © 1996, 2004. Used by permission of Tyndale House Publishers, Inc., Carol Stream, Illinois 60188. All rights reserved.

Scripture quotations marked NIV are taken from the *Holy Bible,* New International Version®. NIV®. Copyright © 1973, 1978, 1984 by International Bible Society. Used by permission of Zondervan. All rights reserved.

ISBN-13: 978-1-4143-1477-8
ISBN-10: 1-4143-1477-9

Printed in China

13 12 11 10 09 08 07
 7   6   5   4   3   2   1

Hopes and Dreams

We are God's masterpiece. He has created us anew in Christ Jesus, so we can do the good things he planned for us long ago.   Ephesians 2:10

As the clock rounds midnight and another year closes, a new year rushes to greet us. A new 365 days are waiting to fulfill our hopes and dreams. In this new beginning, we can receive each day like a gift waiting to be unwrapped. Discover the possibilities by becoming more aware of God's great love for you.

God has made you unique, unlike anyone else in history. You are a precious individual, with gifts that no one else can offer. You are a masterpiece of the master Creator, who longs for you to become the person he made you to be.

Does this new year hold new beginnings, a new path toward fulfilled dreams? Only you can set your goals and chart your course. Write down your intentions and hang them on your mirror. Talk to God about your hopes, for God's desire is to bless you as you live out the dreams he has placed in your heart.

Unwrap the gift of the present by living your dreams!

Out of the Icy Rut

Anyone who belongs to Christ has become a new person. The old life is gone; a new life has begun!
2 Corinthians 5:17

I was entranced. As I rose quietly above the snow-covered treetops, the serenity of the Rockies captivated me. The air was crisp and clean, the sky was blue, and the snow glittered like a dusting of diamonds. Skiing down each powdery run was an adventure.

This time, about halfway down, my skis locked up. They were pointing straight down . . . in a rut. My brain kept telling my legs to turn, but my skis did not respond. Then I fell. My equipment kept racing to the bottom of the next hill, so I was surprised when my skidding, snow-covered body came to a rest on a mogul below.

In our lives, we must decide to make every day count. If we do not intentionally choose to enjoy each day, our lives too quickly get stuck in a rut.

We are made new in Christ. Through him, we are able to enjoy life fully. Point your path away from life's ruts. Dream big, and make the most of every day.

Break a new trail.

Joy Is a Choice

This is the day the LORD has made. We will rejoice and be glad in it.
                                                   Psalm 118:24

Toddlers are interesting little creatures. It doesn't take much experience with two-year-olds to realize that their main concern is with themselves. "Me" is everything, and "me" is great until something happens that wasn't the toddler's idea—such as a diaper change or being buckled into a car seat.

As adults, we sometimes have similar dysfunctions. Life is great until it doesn't go our way. When we don a bad attitude in response, we encounter a dilemma. Life is meant to be celebrated, with each day lived as a gift. Yet most days we act as if we have nothing at all to be glad about.

God gives us each day, asks us if we will rejoice in it, and leaves the choice to us. The outcome of each part of our lives comes down to a daily choice of attitude. If we choose joy and thankfulness, each day becomes a priceless treasure. If we remain focused on ourselves, our world will close in on us. Take up the once-in-a-lifetime opportunity to enjoy the gift of today.

Choose joy today!

Something out of Nothing

O LORD, you are our Father. We are the clay, and you are the potter. We all are formed by your hand.

Isaiah 64:8

One thing I love about life is being able to make something new from whatever materials are on hand. Take, for instance, the ability to begin with a blank canvas and add a few colors to make a beautiful painting. We can combine scraps of fabric to create a beautiful quilt, or raise a beautiful garden out of dirt and a few seeds. We can take simple things and make them into something that previously did not exist.

God is the master Creator of all that exists. He causes a seed to grow into something grand from a patch of dirt, a sprinkle of water, and some sunshine. God also wants to transform our lives into something beautiful, one day at a time. The master Creator wants to take the raw materials of our lives and continually mold us into something new and beautiful. Each new day, God invites us to fuller lives as we allow him to shape us.

Work with God to give your life a beautiful new shape today.

A Little Winter Color

Think about the things of heaven, not the things of earth.
Colossians 3:2

Every year in early January, colorful garden catalogs begin arriving in my snow-covered mailbox. In the bleakest days of the year, garden lovers like me long for a little color. If we can't see beautiful flowers in the backyard, we pore over plant catalogs to nourish our light- and color-deprived eyes. It is refreshing to think about beautiful gardens in the middle of winter.

Just as I take joy in planning my garden in the dark days of winter, my heart is refreshed as I fix my thoughts on God. When we focus on God, we gain his perspective on our earthly problems. As we see our lives through his eyes, we realize that the God who created heaven and earth holds the circumstances of our lives close to his heart.

Setting our minds on lovely things brightens our outlook and colors our world. As we meditate on God and his goodness, our lives will reflect his joy. Resting secure in God's love, we can reflect God's light into the lives of others.

Set your eyes on heavenly things and fill your life with joy.

The Presence of God

The LORD is close to the brokenhearted; he rescues those whose spirits are crushed. The righteous person faces many troubles, but the LORD comes to the rescue each time.
Psalm 34:18-19

After the Christmas unwrapping, a few gifts usually need to be returned or exchanged. Long lines at every store make each return a chore. One year, I received a leopard-print sweater from a well-meaning loved one. The thought and effort invested in the gift touched me, but I knew that I would never wear it—it just wasn't me.

Gifts can be very hard to select. We want our loved ones to like what we have picked out. God probably feels the same way. He gives us so many gifts—our next heartbeat, the frosty design on the window, a laugh shared with a friend—and he wants us to enjoy each one. He especially hopes that we will never reject the gift of his presence.

God's presence empowers us when we feel weak, and it enables us to soar when we feel weighed down. God comforts our broken hearts and rescues us when we feel trapped. We can experience God's presence by simply opening our hearts to him. He is always there.

God's presence is his gift to us.

The Gift of Generosity

Give freely and become more wealthy; be stingy and lose everything. The generous will prosper; those who refresh others will . . . be refreshed. Proverbs 11:24-25

Soon after the Christmas cards stop coming, the Christmas bills begin to arrive. Giving is costly, regardless of the price tag. Yet God says that in giving of ourselves and in focusing on others, we will be refreshed.

Many aspects of life seem contradictory. Solomon's statement in Proverbs 11 points to one such paradox that is hard to wrap our minds around. From the time we were children experimenting with water in the tub, we learned that a certain amount of water put in a cup is the amount that comes back out. Apparently, God's math is a little different from ours, for he says that as we pour ourselves out for others, we will get back even more. God says that our resources in him are unlimited—we can give and give and still have more to give.

As we practice generosity with our energy, time, and money, we enjoy God's blessing and refreshment. Generosity, it seems, is a freeing gift from God.

Give generously; God will fill you back up.

Snowplow Mountains

If you have faith as small as a mustard seed, you can say to this mountain, "Move from here to there" and it will move. Nothing will be impossible for you.

Matthew 17:20, NIV

In the Midwest, we often have large January snows. Some winters we receive only dustings, but other winters we are up to our knees in drifts. One memorable January brought huge quantities of snow. It seemed that every spare moment for weeks was spent clearing the driveway so we could use it. I clearly remember working to clear the drive . . . and the sinking feeling as the snowplow returned. As some of you know, one pass from the plow pushes a mountain of snow onto the end of the drive—which meant that just as I thought I had finished, I had to begin again.

The attitudes and behaviors we work hard to remove from our lives can resurface in the blink of an eye. Just when we think we've overcome anger, for example, the "snowplow" is back with another load. The Bible tells us not to despair. Though the mountain seems impossible to move, we can do it with God's strength.

Nothing is impossible for God.

Stacking a Snowman

*Don't store up treasures here on earth. . . . Store
your treasures in heaven, where moths and rust
cannot destroy, and thieves do not break in and steal.
Wherever your treasure is, there the desires of your
heart will also be.* Matthew 6:19-21

Winter fun comes in all forms at our house: sledding, snow
forts, snow angels, snow cream, and the favorite—snow-
men. We love to gather up old hats and mittens, sunglasses
and scarves, to decorate our carefully stacked men. A tall,
long-lasting snowman always has a big foundation ball and
progressively smaller balls ascending to the top.

So it must be in our lives—the strongest part must be
the foundation. A strong relationship with Jesus must come
first if we are to have a meaningful, eternal life. Jesus said
that our lives are balanced when God is our treasure, but if
we build our lives on money, houses, clothes, or power, it
will all wash away. Putting God first brings the deep satisfaction and contentment of a lasting investment.

As we seek to know God's desires in all that we do, our
lives will grow and flourish as we rest on the strong foundation of God's love.

For a fulfilled life, store your treasures in heaven.

On a Great Team

Have faith in God.   Mark 11:22

Each January, the world watches with great anticipation and celebration as a display of self-sacrifice, discipline, and teamwork lights up living-room TV screens. We watch with delight the competition for the title in professional football: the Super Bowl. As a nation, we are inspired by the passion and skills displayed for the benefit of the team.

In life, we can choose to be on God's team. God gave each of us talents and skills that he wants us to use to passionately impact our world.

To be most effective, we need daily contact with God in prayer. As he calls the plays, we must faithfully follow his directions. When we respond wholeheartedly to his calls, our lives will be effective. Just as touchdowns are scored by a team working together, our lives gain significance as we work together with God and others.

When we act in faith to the best of our ability, God works behind the scenes to pull things together. Being on God's team means responding when God calls the plays and trusting him for the outcome. Together, we can touch the world.

We team up with a mighty God.

Snowflakes

What are mere mortals that you should think about them, human beings that you should care for them? Yet you made them only a little lower than God and crowned them with glory and honor. Psalm 8:4-5

Some of life's greatest blessings come from slowing down. When we live life at a slower pace, we regain perspective and see ourselves more as Jesus sees us. In opening our eyes to the beauty that surrounds us in nature, we learn more about God's miraculous love and creation. One beautiful winter wonder is found in the intricacy of snowflakes. Simply catching snowflakes on a black surface showcases them like diamonds on black velvet.

In our finite minds, it is hard to imagine the infinite variety of snowflakes, but God must take pleasure in the simple, delicate beauty of each one. How much more God values each human life! He fashions and creates each individual and takes great pleasure in our delicate lives. How incredible!

Through our own wonder, we learn volumes about our awesome Creator. We gain fresh perspective as we discover the magnificence of our God.

Appreciate God's beautiful handiwork!

Preparing for a New Season

No one puts new wine into old wineskins. For the old skins would burst from the pressure, spilling the wine and ruining the skins. New wine is stored in new wineskins so that both are preserved. Matthew 9:17

For me, one of the hardest holiday jobs is putting away the decorations. The special ornaments that help us celebrate Jesus' birth are a treasured part of Christmas, but as we hang the calendar for a new year, it is time to put them away.

At our house, the lights come off the tree in one big, hopeless tangle. Decorations never fit back into their boxes—I always need at least one more. Nonetheless, it is time to take down the old things and prepare for a new season.

In Matthew 9, Jesus speaks about the perils of putting new wine into old containers. Our lives, made new by believing in him, are like the new wine. If we are to be effective, our newness should not be folded back into our old habits, attitudes, and routines. Instead, we should clean out our old ways and make room for the new life that God is leading us to.

Learn new ways to live and serve.

Frost-Free Driving

Let us strip off every weight that slows us down, especially the sin that so easily trips us up.   Hebrews 12:1

When our family moved to the Midwest from the Deep South, we had to make many adjustments. We were glad to give up swarming termites, kudzu, and oppressive heat, but we weren't quite ready for the winter snow and ice. Winter wasn't a problem, of course, until we had to go somewhere. All of us have learned the hard way not to be in too much of a hurry in defrosting the windshield. Driving off with a frosty windshield is like driving with our eyes closed.

God does not want us to drive blind. We need to rid ourselves of whatever hinders us, like scraping off the windshield before we drive down life's road. Blocked vision makes us ineffective and interferes with God's desires for us. Jesus said, "My purpose is to give them a rich and satisfying life" (John 10:10). He wants our lives to be fulfilling and rewarding.

As we pursue the life Jesus intends for us, we need to give up whatever relationships, habits, commitments, values, or activities keep us from a full and rich relationship with God.

Remove whatever blocks your way to God.

Chickadee Feeder

Wherever the Spirit of the Lord is, there is freedom.
2 Corinthians 3:17

To get through the winter doldrums, I enjoy feeding the birds. The red cardinals are delightful, and the chickadees practice their lively flight just outside our window. One year, we hung a circular feeder with large cathedral windows. One day when it was empty, a tiny chickadee slipped under the glass in search of seed. I worked hard in the frozen air to encourage the trapped chickadee back out. If it was difficult for the bird to squeeze into the feeder, it was even harder for it to exit, but it eventually flew away.

God probably watches us become trapped by various aspects of life: a hard-to-break habit, an abusive relationship, a financial burden, a dead-end job. We somehow manage to squeeze into situations that look good from the outside, and then we are unable to free ourselves.

When the events of our lives hold us captive, God calls us to freedom. Jesus paid our way out of life's traps when he gave his life for ours on the cross. When we trust him, we begin to clearly see the route to freedom. Trust God to set you free today.

Jesus sets us free.

Season's First Snowdrop

I will praise the LORD at all times. I will constantly speak his praises.
Psalm 34:1

Moving at breakneck speed often causes us to miss out on life's beauty. In the midst of my scurrying one January day, uncommon beauty caught my eye. In the melting snow by the front walk was the first snowdrop of the season. I can still see it in my mind's eye, with its delicate white petals unfolding from green stems just above the snow-covered ground.

That day I learned that even in the middle of challenges and hardships, busyness, and unexpected news, our lives can be like the snowdrop, blooming beautifully in the cold and snow.

None of us know what tomorrow will bring. God has called us to praise and thank him for the precious gift of life today. He invites us to slow down and soak in the miracles that bloom around us. Be fully present to the beauty of a delicate flower, the padding pajama-feet of freshly bathed kids, and laughter shared with loved ones.

In the coming year, praise God each day for the miracles and the simple joys of life.

Pause to appreciate the miracles of life.

Healthy Balance

God's temple is holy, and you are that temple.

1 Corinthians 3:17

January is a busy time for health clubs and fitness centers, as Americans deal with post-holiday pounds and honor New Year's fitness resolutions.

Jesus spent much of his life healing the sick, physically and spiritually. Jesus demonstrates that our physical and spiritual well-being should be a top priority and that the health of body and soul are invariably related. Remember the last time you liked the way you looked, inside and outside?

To change our quality of life, we must make conscious choices and practice them until they become habits. Imagine taking small steps throughout the year toward a healthier you!

Experts recommend getting thirty minutes of exercise a few times per week, eating fresher, less processed foods, and getting a good night's sleep. In addition, setting aside a few minutes daily to connect with God in silent reflection, prayer, and Bible reading will strengthen us from the inside out. By taking small steps, we can achieve a healthy balance that helps us to be at our best. God will meet us in our goals, empower us to follow through, and fill our lives with love and joy.

God cares about our physical and spiritual health.

Matching Hearts

God created human beings in his own image.

Genesis 1:27

It is fun to talk with married couples and hear stories about how they met. Some met on blind dates, in college classes, or at work, and some were high school sweethearts. Usually couples discover some funny coincidence after they meet, like growing up in the same church or town without knowing each other. As they grow together in marriage, couples gain matching hearts.

The same principle applies to us with God. Before we were born, God formed each of us to reflect his image. As we begin to know him, we realize that our hearts are made from the same mold as his. Like him, we were born to love, to delight, to create, and to live fully day by day. We look at many worldly things, trying to find a satisfying match for our hearts, but without God in our lives, we are incomplete, dissatisfied, and still searching.

As humans, we are meant to be in relationship with God. Our souls are made for his. Our lives are only complete and fulfilled as we get to know Jesus. As we grow in spirit, our hearts become more like his.

God matched our hearts perfectly to his.

A Road Map for the Way

The LORD directs the steps of the godly. He delights in every detail of their lives.   Psalm 37:23

Each year, our family likes to set off cross-country to explore new places via a road trip. Of course, whether we're passing over mountains, navigating the coast, or crossing the plains, the key to every unfamiliar journey is to have a good map.

Just as new destinations are best located by a road map, each unfamiliar day is best begun with guidance. In the Bible, God has provided us with a reliable road map for our lives. The more we study and absorb his Word, the more familiar our course will become. Even when life's hills seem higher and the road more winding than we expected, we can be encouraged. God has written about his love and recorded the journeys of those who have gone before us to give us patience and endurance along the way.

If your journey is tough, hang in there! The destination God has in mind will be worth the trouble. Connect daily with the Mapmaker and study the road map he has created.

God directs us as we seek his way.

Sharing the Warmth

When God's people are in need, be ready to help them.
Always be eager to practice hospitality.   Romans 12:13

In a world that treasures domestic perfection and encourages faultless home entertaining, it is hard to open our hearts and homes to others. However, Jesus does not tell us to be hospitable according to a particular name brand or standard of perfection, but by opening our hearts and homes to others.

Instead of concentrating on perfectly appointed décor, just relax in a comfortable retreat where smiles abound and laughter rings out, bringing the greatest memories and rewards. The best times can take place across a garage sale table while sharing simple macaroni and cheese. True warmth and good hospitality do not require place cards. They can best be found in a warm smile to a stranger at the store, a kind word for a hurting soul, a generous meal shared with someone who is hungry, or a hearty welcome for a visiting neighbor.

Take a step of faith and invite a friend for a cup of coffee; enjoy the simple joy of sharing your life with another.

God wants us to open our hearts and homes.

Winter Sunrise

May those who love you rise like the sun in all its power!
                                                    Judges 5:31

Early one winter morning, the rosy light coming through the windows got my attention. I slipped on a coat and hat and grabbed my camera, for this was not a sunrise to be ignored. In the backyard away from the disruption of neighboring houses, I stood in awe of the colorful clouds rolling across the sky before my eyes. I attempted to capture their vibrant beauty and majesty on film that morning, but no photograph could convey the vastness of that brief, spectacular scene.

The colorful beauty of the sunrise quietly displays the great Artist's love for the waking world. Each sunrise is a love letter sent to each of us, emblazoned with God's power and signed by his deep love. Our lives would change for the better if we really perceived our Creator's deep love.

Today, and each day this year, begin your day with a prayer. Before your feet hit the floor, commit your direction, attitude, and outlook for the day to God. In the love that God gives, your life will shine like the sunrise to illumine the world with his love and joy.

God paints his love in each sunrise.

A Most Important Gift

Children are a gift from the LORD; they are a reward from him.   Psalm 127:3

Recently, our oldest child brought an invitation home from school. It said, "Please join me for a celebration of my writings at school. Refreshments will be served." We hung the invitation on the refrigerator and marked it on our calendars.

At the celebration, one child was clearly distraught when no one came to celebrate with him. This child lives in the town's wealthiest neighborhood, and his parents drive the nicest cars to their high-powered jobs. However, they missed the opportunity of a lifetime to celebrate their child's accomplishments and encourage him.

As adults, it is hard for us to step into a child's world. We are caught up in our hardworking worlds and sometimes miss the things that matter most. Our relationships will last for eternity, and treasured memories last forever in our hearts. The money in our bank accounts hardly lasts to the end of the month.

As you work hard to deposit money at the bank, deposit encouragement into the lives of those you love. Make time today to treasure the most important gifts in your life. Give of yourself in the manner appreciated most—through the gift of time.

Show your loved ones that you care.

Loving When It's Hard

Imitate God . . . in everything you do, because you are his dear children. Live a life filled with love, following the example of Christ.   Ephesians 5:1-2

Do you remember the last time you settled into a cozy corner with a page-turner for the last ten minutes of your lunch break, to unwind after a hectic morning? Did your new coworker interrupt you with one more question about a procedure she still didn't understand?

Showing mercy when we don't feel like it is a very hard thing to do. In theory, we love to help others, but when love extends beyond our comfort zone into self-sacrifice, it is very difficult.

In Ephesians 5, we are told to use Christ's life as a pattern for our own. Jesus always had someone waiting and wanting more from him. In Matthew 15, we see the disciples shooing away a persistent woman. Instead of seeming put out, Jesus heaped on a double dose of compassion and helped her with her need.

Like Jesus, we can give of ourselves even when it is inconvenient, especially to our loved ones. Extending a bit more care to meet someone's need can make their day.

Shine a little love on others.

The View from Our Side

"Don't be afraid!" Elisha told him. "For there are more on our side than on theirs!" . . . *The LORD opened the young man's eyes, and when he looked up, he saw that the hillside around Elisha was filled with horses and chariots of fire.*　　　　2 Kings 6:16-17

In modern life, we rely on many things to work when we need them. We trust that the brakes on our cars will function when we need to stop. We don't check them every day to see if they are still there—we just trust our lives to their effectiveness whenever we drive.

Although God says that he will always be there for us, it is sometimes hard to feel his presence. Elisha was surrounded by two attacking armies, and his servant was overwhelmed by the number of enemy soldiers (see 2 Kings 6). When God opened the servant's eyes, he saw that the Lord's army far outnumbered their enemies. God already had everything under control.

God's help in our daily lives is more reliable than our car's brakes. There is nothing to fear. God has everything in his hands, and all we have to do is trust.

Call on God, knowing that he is present.

We're Not Home Alone

The disciples . . . woke him up, shouting, "Lord, save us! We're going to drown!" Jesus responded, "Why are you afraid? You have so little faith!" Then he got up and rebuked the wind and waves, and suddenly there was a great calm. Matthew 8:25-26

From our own forgetfulness, and from watching the parents in *Home Alone* forget their child when they went on vacation, it is easy to think that God may also overlook his responsibilities—such as caring for our lives. The endlessly searching for a new job, longing to conceive a baby, continued suffering of physical ailments—all raise questions. Where is God? How long will I have to suffer? Has God forgotten me?

The disciples were caught in a violent storm as they crossed the Sea of Galilee. Jesus was sleeping, and the disciples wondered why he wasn't concerned like they were. When they cried out, "Lord, save us!" Jesus answered, "Why are you afraid?" Although the storm was raging and they felt that they would die, God had not abandoned them and would not let them drown.

Nor will God let us drown in the midst of our storms. He will calm the wind and the waves in our lives when we trust him.

Jesus can calm your storms.

Trail Ride

"I know the plans I have for you," says the L<small>ORD</small>. *"They are plans for good and not for disaster, to give you a future and a hope."*
Jeremiah 29:11

For a few years, I grew up down South, deep in the heart of Texas. In cowgirl tradition, I donned pigtails, a thick accent, and sometimes a cowgirl hat. One of those times was at a friend's birthday party, where we were invited for a trail ride on the friendly ranch horses. I loved to ride, so I mounted and took off.

Normally, a horse obliges by following its rider's lead. That day, before I could gather my voice to holler, we were off at a full canter, wildly pursuing my horse's agenda. Luckily, we soon reached his favorite destination—the barn.

Sometimes, our everyday lives are a wild ride. In following God's lead, we realize that God will do the best job of arranging the details of our lives, leaving us with less need to worry and more time to enjoy what he has provided. When we let God lead, we will find in abundance whatever else we were looking for as well.

Rest your plans in God's hands.

The Cheap Fountain

Jesus Christ is the same yesterday, today, and forever.
Hebrews 13:8

One winter, I bought a lovely outdoor fountain for a great price. Come spring, the fountain looked and sounded beautiful in our garden—I loved it! As the days passed, however, the pump slowed and the powder-coated finish chipped. Within weeks, the fountain did not work at all. What a disappointment!

In life, we look for meaning in much the same way that we spend our money. We take the least expensive route and hope to get the best things. We hope that cheap emotional substitutes will fill the enormous chasm in our hearts. We believe that working harder, acquiring more things, filling our days, and sedating our deep needs will quiet our longings. After a time, we realize that we are not finding satisfaction; only God fulfills our desire for real purpose.

God doesn't wear out, fade away, quit working, or become a burden. Cheap substitutes may make us happy for a while, but in the end they disappoint. True fulfillment of our deepest longings comes only from the stability of God's love.

The book of Hebrews tells us that Jesus Christ is unchanging. We can find lasting significance and joy in knowing that his love will never end.

God's love never changes.

The Presence of a Smile

The LORD is my strength and shield. I trust him with all my heart. He helps me, and my heart is filled with joy. I burst out in songs of thanksgiving. Psalm 28:7

A dear friend of mine always inspires me to smile more. The room brightens as she enters. Laura has every reason not to smile—she lost her husband at a young age, raised her four boys by herself, and this year, as a grandma, she is battling cancer. As she endures her fourth round of chemotherapy, she does not complain, but radiates the smile of a woman held dear by her heavenly Father. Laura says that she smiles because she thinks about God's blessings rather than her circumstances.

It is hard to smile in the face of hardships, but life in our world will always include struggle. As we go through each challenge, we have a choice: We can either focus on God's goodness and trust him with the hard stuff, or we can focus on our problems and miss out on life's joys. When our lives are focused on God, we cannot keep from smiling.

Focus on life's blessings.

Worried and Wondering

Don't worry about anything; instead, pray about everything. Tell God what you need, and thank him for all he has done. Then you will experience God's peace, which exceeds anything we can understand.

Philippians 4:6-7

Life has many unknowns. Mothers must let their children leave for their first day of preschool, first bus ride, first sleepover, first drive behind the wheel, first date, first day of college. . . . We may worry about keeping our job, getting the promotion, making a go of our small business, or having enough money to see us through retirement. There are so many things to worry about.

As a nation, we are very good at being anxious. There are so many unknowns. Just a few minutes tuned to a news network will give us plenty more to worry about: the latest terrorist threats, flu outbreaks, traffic accidents, health scares.

We don't know what tomorrow, or even the next moment, will bring. Thankfully, we know who holds each day and moment. Paul writes, "Don't worry about anything." He can say this because God has every issue under his control. Our part is to pray and trust; God will give us peace beyond our understanding. Turn off the news and trust God in everything.

Trust God with your needs.

Covering the Roses

Let all who take refuge in you rejoice; let them sing joyful praises forever. Spread your protection over them, that all who love your name may be filled with joy.

Psalm 5:11

I fell in love with the roses the second my husband and I walked into the backyard of our first house. One rose-bush was red and the other pink. Because this was in New Orleans, I did not have to do anything to keep those roses alive; they simply bloomed. When we moved to the Midwest, I started a garden in our backyard by planting a few roses. I didn't know to cover them for the winter, so they died that season. Roses in our Midwest climate need the snow for protection against the extreme winter cold, and it helps if we cover them too. Now, years later, I have lost a few, but I enjoy many thriving roses in our gardens.

Like the snow that covers the winter roses, God covers our lives with his protection. He knows our needs before we do. God's love and protection come quietly, like the first snowflake falling. His sovereign hand may be hard to perceive, but unlike the world's security systems, God will never fail us. His presence fills us with joy.

God shelters our lives.

Sled-Pulling Exhaustion

In quietness and confidence is your strength.

Isaiah 30:15

Winter always brings a favorite sport at our house. When the first snow falls, our boxer, Jesse, knows her role. We walk the toboggan onto the snow-covered street, load the kids up one-two-three on the sled, and Jesse pulls it away. Dogs love productive work, and Jesse feels useful when she pulls the sled. She goes untiringly all over the neighborhood until she wears herself out. Then she's done, kaput.

Surely God looks down on us as we go about our little routines in such a frenzy, wondering why we make life such hard work. Perhaps, like Jesse, we need to feel useful. It is easy to fill up the schedule with activities, and then to fill it up even more, to make us feel worthwhile. Our hurry does not make our lives any richer. We just keep cramming more in until we are exhausted.

God says that quietness gives us confidence and strength. We were made for calmness, not craziness. Instead of wearing yourself out, take a few minutes to replenish your spirit with the Lord. He will restore you.

God gives us quiet strength and confidence.

Rest by the Fire

Jesus said, "Let's go off by ourselves to a quiet place and rest awhile."

Mark 6:31

Winter is a time for rest. From bears to butterflies, deciduous trees to summer's flowers, nature takes a break in the winter. When we sit by the fire, play board games, or read a book, the time taken for reflection refreshes and renews our spirits. When a fire warms our hands and feet, it also warms our souls. Winter rest by the fire is important—we all need to slow down and recharge.

I am thankful to know that Jesus needed to rest at times. Jesus was fully human, so he needed refreshment, just as we do. He took the disciples aside to refresh and renew their spirits. God also rested from his work of creation to reflect on what he had made.

It is easy for us to keep going without slowing down. Without time to reflect on where we've been or evaluate where we are headed, we easily lose perspective. Our lives are much more effective when we take time for recreation and reflection.

This winter, sit by the fire and enjoy some rest.

Take time for rest.

Who We Are

I am the LORD, your God, the Holy One of Israel, your Savior. . . . You are precious to me. You are honored, and I love you.   Isaiah 43:3-4

The middle-school years are a hard part of growing up, for a young teenager's self-worth is based on the opinions of others. I was extra tall and gangly, with a metal-mouthed smile. I tried to wear the right clothes and not be too smart, but I was never in the "in" crowd.

So much of what we do is based on what we imagine others want from us. However, all that we strive to be and do in pleasing others is still rarely enough.

God takes us "as is" and loves each of us for who we are. We can do nothing to make him love us more or less. God knows that we are not perfect, but to him, we are precious, honored, and loved.

Feast on the richness of God's love today. Allow this truth to saturate your life: God loves me for who I am. His perfect love will transform your days.

God loves us for who we are.

Larger Loving

Live a life filled with love, following the example of Christ.
                                                                    Ephesians 5:2

Some people are easy to love, such as the huggable baby on the television ad who coos and smiles, never has a dirty diaper, and never makes a mess. The perfect people we conjure up in our minds are easy to love, but in real life, no one is perfect.

Sometimes it is hardest to show love to those we really love the most. At work and in our social lives, it is easy to put on a smile and a mask that hides our true selves. When we get home and take the mask off, our true selves show through. Our families often get the raw edges of our hearts, the rough places that we hide in public.

It is hard to love others on our own. Yet when we are tired, disappointed, frustrated, and harassed, we can draw on Jesus' love to help us love our families. God's strength and love are enough, but we have to ask for his help.

The only way to love others is to receive love from God. Ask Jesus to enlarge your loving heart today!

Grow in love.

Hard-to-Love Neighbors

Love each other with genuine affection, and take delight in honoring each other.   Romans 12:10

Daily life allows us to cross paths with many types of people. Though most of us prefer being around fun-loving people, we all encounter people who make life much more difficult. Be it the quick-to-judge neighbor with the perfectly manicured lawn or the coworker engrossed only in bettering her bottom line, certain people offer criticism freely and belittle others who don't measure up.

Following Jesus by honoring others instead of being quick to criticize is unnatural for humans. However, we can learn to honor others by allowing them to be themselves and by putting ourselves in their shoes before we criticize. If we are not perfect, how can we pass judgment on others?

With the help of God's love, we can encourage our children to uncover their God-given interests without forcing our own ideas on them. We can learn to see our neighbors through God's eyes. God will help us to love our spouses even when they come home late or leave their socks on the floor. Genuine love and honor can replace self-interest and bring delight and joy to each day.

God helps us to love difficult people.

Yielding the Right-of-Way

Submit to one another out of reverence for Christ.
Ephesians 5:21

Remember learning to drive? Once you mastered driving on city streets, your instructor probably took you onto the interstate. Driving on the highway is pretty straightforward, except for the on-ramps. Entering a highway is difficult even for seasoned drivers because traffic is already traveling full speed, and there isn't always room to merge. It is difficult to yield while still moving forward.

Yielding is an important quality in loving relationships. To yield is to consider others' feelings before you make your own move. The advice in Ephesians 5 for marriage and other relationships is controversial today, but it still applies.

It isn't easy to submit. In a marriage, unless you consider your husband's feelings as well as your own, your relationship will crash. When you yield as a wife to your husband, you build his love and respect toward you. In contrast, if you force your opinions and plow through each day wanting only your own way, your husband's respect for you will fade. As you merge your life in various relationships, you yield your own rights to encourage love and prevent relational disasters.

Today, yield your own rights for the good of another to reach your destination safely.

Consider another's feelings alongside your own.

Peanut Butter Blessings

A real friend sticks closer than a brother.   Proverbs 18:24

Oh the joy and serendipity of a friend's presence! Unplanned gatherings brighten even bleak wintry days with the warmth of friendship. Opening our lives and our schedules to an impromptu PB and J lunch brings the blessing of deepening friendships. Time spent with friends can enrich our lives with spontaneous laughter and fond memories.

Sometimes we are stretched so thin that we miss out on the best parts of life. Women need female friends. Though our spouses may be very supportive, they can never play the role of a girlfriend. For some reason, men don't have the same passion for scrapbooks and fabric swatches, recipes and bargains, so God gave us the wonderful gift of girlfriends. Whether going shopping, having coffee, or doing crafts, we can share our joys and encourage one another in our heartaches through the blessing of friendships.

We are not self-sufficient. Especially in the midst of our normally busy, wired, and disconnected world, we need friends that stick close to us through tough times. The sharing of burdens and joys in friendship makes life much richer. Through close friends, we give and receive the gift of God's encouragement. With real friends, life comes to life!

Slow down and be a great friend!

A New Day Dawning

Choose today whom you will serve. . . . But as for me and my family, we will serve the Lord. Joshua 24:15

When we rise, we must choose the day's direction.

Choice 1: It's 5:36 a.m. and the alarm is sounding . . . already. The day's burdens seem overwhelming, and I am defeated before my feet even hit the floor. I don't see the beautiful sunrise—I only perceive obstacles and problems. Today will be a hard day. . . .

Choice 2: It's 5:36 a.m. and the alarm is ringing. As I awake, I am aware of how much I have to be thankful for. God is present and in control, and I choose to trust God's love. I see the beautiful sunrise and focus on the new day and its possibilities. Many responsibilities vie for my attention, so I begin the day with prayer, telling God my concerns and asking for his peace, joy, and guidance.

God's plan is for us to live fully and abundantly, freed by his love. Will you serve God and receive his gift of life, or go it alone in your own limited strength? Choose life today!

Celebrate the precious gift of life!

The Gift of Today

Our days on earth are like grass; like wildflowers, we bloom and die. The wind blows, and we are gone—as though we had never been here.   Psalm 103:15-16

This time of year, the grass, fields, and trees are still a drab brown. The days are beginning to warm up, but most of nature is still sleeping. The crocuses are gradually poking their heads up to face the rising sun. In purples, whites, yellows, and striped blues, they smile and bless the world with their beauty. But their beauty is soon gone. We must enjoy it today!

If we live to be one hundred, our lives will still feel short. There will never be enough days for us to do and be all that we hope for. Busyness hustles us along, and we slip into routines. Days come and go with little to show for them.

God gives each of us the incredible gift of today's opportunities! Today has every ingredient needed for making a difference to others. We don't know what lies just around the bend, and there are no guarantees for tomorrow. But today has infinite value. Let's be fully alive and enjoy the gift of today!

Live the gift of today.

Only Dust

The LORD is like a father to his children, tender and compassionate to those who fear him. For he knows how weak we are; he remembers we are only dust.
Psalm 103:13-14

I was very young when I started taking piano lessons, and in grade school I began to play the viola, a great match for my long fingers. I quickly learned the difficulty of playing stringed instruments. The piano always hits a note at the right pitch, but how a stringed instrument sounds is completely dependent on where the finger is placed. The pitch of each note is very hard to get right, and it normally sounds a little screechy. Practice helps tremendously, but it probably never makes perfect.

In life, we try to hit the right pitch and make a pleasing sound with our lives. Though practice doesn't make life perfect, God delights in our best efforts as we learn, grow, and become more of who he made us to be.

God hears our screechy attempts at living. He knows that we are beginners, and he loves us just the same. Be your best today, knowing that God accepts you for who you are.

God doesn't expect perfection.

Chill for the Tulips

The LORD is compassionate and merciful, slow to get angry and filled with unfailing love.   Psalm 103:8

As the sprouting bulbs emerge silently from the thawing earth, they bring the color and fragrance of spring. Tulips and daffodils know to bloom when they've had their prescribed period of cold weather. Like the pop-up thermometer in the Thanksgiving turkey, God made his beautiful bulbs to push up when they've had enough winter.

God loves and sustains all of creation. He has compassion on the brown bulbs in the cold and grants them the reprieve of spring, their time to bloom.

Like bulbs, we spend a lot of our lives in less-than-ideal settings. Pressures from work, relationships, and money turn the heat up. At other times, we feel abandoned, alone, and left out in the cold.

God's love is unfailing; he will not abandon us or put us under more pressure than we can bear. God knows that the times of heat and cold allow us to bloom more beautifully.

God is merciful and compassionate. He cares for the flowers, and he cares much more for you and me! Trust that through it all, you will bloom beautifully in his time.

Each of us is beautiful in God's time.

Outstretched Arms

For his unfailing love toward those who fear him is as great as the height of the heavens above the earth. He has removed our sins as far from us as the east is from the west.
Psalm 103:11-12

"So-o-o-o much!" she said, stretching out her arms in response to "How much does daddy love you?" Children are cute as they learn to make sense of their world. My niece knows how much her daddy loves her, but as adults, we often forget how much our heavenly Father cares for us.

The psalmist David's response to "How much does your heavenly Daddy love you?" is "As great as the height of the heavens above the earth!" My small mind has trouble wrapping itself around the infinite distance from here to heaven, but David tells us that God's love for each of us is unending.

God's love for you and me is so great that he cancels all of our wrongs when we are sincerely sorry. God doesn't sweep our sins under the rug for use on a later day. He separates our sins from us as far as the east is from the west.

Train your mind to appreciate how much your heavenly Daddy loves you.

God's love for us is infinite.

God Made It All for You

Oh, that we might know the LORD! Let us press on to know him. He will respond to us as surely as the arrival of dawn or the coming of rains in early spring. Hosea 6:3

We go about our days to the low hum of man-made machines. As our technologies enable us to process things faster, we tend to forget the Creator of life and time. God's plan for our lives is full and rich, even in our fast-paced world.

Whatever the weather, take a walk outside today and observe the beauty of creation. If you were the only person in all of history, God would still have created this big and beautiful world—just for you! He loves each of us so much that he longs to reach out and touch us through creation.

God created the sweet melody of the songbird to grace your ear, the gentle breeze that softly brushes your face, the sweetly scented spring blossoms to perfume your walk, and the refreshing colors of flowers, grass, and sky to bless your vision.

Awaken your senses and appreciate God's great love. Enjoy a walk outdoors and listen to God's love expressed in the voice of creation.

He made it for you!

Crown of Beauty

He will give a crown of beauty for ashes, a joyous blessing instead of mourning. . . . Instead of shame and dishonor, you will enjoy a double share of honor . . . and everlasting joy.　　　　　　　　　　　Isaiah 61:3, 7

On summer days, I enjoy the colorful flower gardens, the lilting flight of the butterflies, the sweet song of the gold finch, the gentle breeze, and the murmur of the fountain. Summer soon passes into the shorter days of fall and then into winter, leaving the gardens bare, brown, and abandoned. Except for birds foraging for seeds, there is little movement. The coneflowers still stand tall into winter, their seeds salvaged for the finches.

One late-winter morning, I discovered a crown of dazzling ice and snow on a brown coneflower head! Such incredible beauty brings joy in the dead of winter.

God brings beauty from our browned and broken souls. He takes our ashen struggles and exchanges them for a delicate crown of beauty. When we come in faith, God gives us his honor and his everlasting joy.

Today, allow God to exchange your ashes for his beauty and joy.

God will free you to joy!

Love Notes and Evening Strolls

Keep on loving each other. Hebrews 13:1

Romance can enrich our lives in the simplest ways.

Let your loved ones know how much you love them. Add a little love to the peanut butter sandwich by sending a note in your child's lunch box. Greet and leave your loved ones with a hug, a kiss, and an "I love you." Instead of spending an evening reading the paper, you could venture outdoors and soak up some God-given beauty. Go for an evening stroll, holding your sweetheart's hand.

Romance requires creativity and an adventurous spirit. Life will not disappoint this type of outlook, and God provides endless experiences for you to enjoy.

Let your romantic side express itself freely today. Make another great memory. Show your love and admiration for those you love. Do something you've always dreamed of doing. Pursue adventure and live fully. Today, slow down and soak up life's loves and simple pleasures.

Take time to show your loved ones that you love them.

Rose Petal Trails

His mouth is sweetness itself; he is desirable in every way. Such . . . is my lover, my friend. Song of Songs 5:16

A close friend and mentor once told me, with a twinkle in her eye, of the plans her husband made for their Valentine's Day. Chocolates and a trail of rose petals through their house brought her to his invitation: a romantic evening of dinner and dancing. They had been through many hard times in their fifty-year marriage, but their love and romance had not faded. She said that their love had sustained them despite the stresses of life because they were mutually committed to expressing their love each day.

On this day for remembering those we love deeply, give something beyond a card. Just as the young woman in the Song of Songs communicates to her beloved, we should show our deep love and appreciation to our loved ones. Have you recently expressed how much you love them? Have you put words to the cute little pleasures of being married to your husband—such as the way he smiles?

Slow down and go out of your way to show all your loved ones how important they are to you. Keep saying "I love you." Your relationships will be enriched.

Express your love today!

Keeping Watch

[God] will not let you stumble; the one who watches over you will not slumber. . . . The LORD keeps you from all harm and watches over your life. Psalm 121:3, 7

A set of baby monitors is a huge blessing for new parents. The monitor transmits peace of mind from the baby's room to the parents' receiver. Many television sitcoms joke about the overuse of the baby monitor, and such stories usually get a big laugh. A paranoid mom wants to hear her baby's every heartbeat, so while she sleeps, she brings the receiver to her nightstand. She turns it to the highest volume and jumps out of her skin when the baby makes the slightest sound. Yes, as women we tend to dote on our loved ones—for safety's sake, of course.

God tells us that he never sleeps as he watches over our lives. What hope and assurance we have in our Lord's protection, day and night! God is the Creator and Life-Giver. We can rest easy in his care. He can move mountains, deter circumstances, or change hearts and minds according to his plan.

We can trust our safety and well-being to our all-powerful Protector.

God watches over our lives.

Good Fences

The LORD is my shepherd; I have all that I need.

Psalm 23:1

Where else but at a zoo can ordinary city-bound folks experience the near proximity of exotic wild animals? We can enjoy the close presence of magnificent animals such as lions because of a zoo's good fences. The boundaries are essential for the safety of visitors, animals, and zookeepers. Because the fences keep the large, wild, and potentially harmful animals in, everyone is free to enjoy their time there.

In life, good fences also make for joyful adventures. Within the protection of a fence, we know our boundaries and are free to explore, learn, and live fully in safety.

David, the writer of Psalm 23, says that God is our Shepherd. Like sheep, we need the guidance and protection of God's boundaries. When we choose to stay with our Shepherd, we have everything we need, because he knows our needs before we do and loves to provide for us. Just as good fences allow for enjoyable experiences, God's guidelines and boundaries found in the Bible help us to live within his protection and care.

Trust God's care, respect his boundaries, and enjoy the adventure of life.

God cares for our every need.

Lupine Meadow

He lets me rest in green meadows; he leads me beside peaceful streams. He renews my strength.   Psalm 23:2-3

One summer, our family vacationed in central Maine's Acadia National Park, located on Mount Desert Island, where mountains rise right out of the ocean. There are lush forests, quaint towns, and a scenic lighthouse. As we drove through one town, an eagle flew overhead. We stopped, and I grabbed my camera and set out after him.

When the eagle disappeared over Somes Sound, something even more majestic captured my attention. At the edge of the sound was a breathtaking field of purple lupine. I stood surrounded by this beauty, enjoying the most peaceful and restful moments of my life. My soul was strengthened and my heart was bursting, as if God had made it just for me.

God knows how to touch our hearts. He gave me a purple lupine meadow. For you, the details will be different, but the feeling will probably be similar: restful, peaceful, enchanting, and laced with love. We don't have to look for such serene moments; we just have to be open to them. God knows our hearts and will lead us to special places of rest.

Open your heart to God's restoration of your body, mind, and spirit.

God restores our strength.

On the Right Track

He guides me along right paths, bringing honor to his name.   Psalm 23:3

I find that trusting God with my life is easy—for about two minutes. Then I get off course and forget the character of the God I trust. Fear sets in, and logic doesn't help.

We can't stay on the right path by ourselves. It sounds funny to say that we need to trust God in order to keep trusting him, but it is true. Only God can give us the faith we need when we ask him for it.

We know that we are on God's path when we check the signposts marking our track. God's Word is a great road map for daily life. It provides wisdom and knowledge about our Lord.

At times, we naturally become impatient with our progress. We think that we should move faster toward our desired destination. As we grow restless, we look for shortcuts that may speed things up. Unfortunately, shortcuts on God's path usually slow us down.

Trust that God is leading you along the right path. He will give you the faith and patience you need. Follow him today—the best is yet to come!

God leads us along his path.

Brighter Hills Ahead

Even when I walk through the darkest valley, I will not be afraid, for you are close beside me. Your rod and your staff protect and comfort me.   Psalm 23:4

I recently indulged my love of painting by taking lessons from a local artist. The best lesson was watching the artist work on her canvas. She skillfully used lights and darks to create highlights and shadows. The bright colors were important, but darker shades helped lighten the highlights and brought the painting to life.

We all have dark, gloomy valleys to walk through. Tragedy strikes us all, through broken relationships, lost jobs, rebellious children, loss of loved ones, or natural disasters. Through our shattered dreams and crushed loves, God holds us close. He is beside us through each long, dark valley.

A life can't shine as brightly without its contrasting shadows. The master Painter allows the dark places of life to give our colors their richness and depth. He has the answers to our many questions. For now, we can rest assured that his faithful presence and healing comfort are all that we need. There are brighter days ahead!

God comforts and protects us.

A Cup Quite Full

You prepare a feast for me in the presence of my enemies. You honor me by anointing my head with oil. My cup overflows with blessings. Psalm 23:5

Our family tends to get sick in late February, as often happens with children in the house. I dread having our home invaded by sneezing, coughing, and sleepless nights, but I realize that God sometimes uses sickness to slow us down. Being home sick is a great time to refuel our spirits and show our love by caring for loved ones.

We can learn to see through Jesus' eyes and realize that regardless of a broken dishwasher, a flat tire, or the family being sick, he is in control. Jesus uses every circumstance in our lives to form us into who he wants us to be. As we choose to see the flowers instead of the weeds, we can see our blessings and be thankful, even during hard times.

Practice having a thankful heart today. Focus on the numerous joys and blessings that sprinkle down with the rain instead of just longing for sunny days. Our glasses are overflowing with God's love.

God blesses our lives.

Sand Castles and Seashells

Surely your goodness and unfailing love will pursue me all the days of my life, and I will live in the house of the LORD *forever.*   Psalm 23:6

Worldwide, people love to vacation at the beach. In our family's favorite spot, we can "leave our shoes at the door" and let the sand rub away our rough edges. The salt water restores our spirits as we pass our days building sand castles, digging large holes, catching blue crabs, and watching dolphins. Through sunsets and shells, footprints and kite-flying, we experience God's pleasure. I love these memories.

God has planted in each of us the longing for a better place than this earth. He made us that way for a reason. If we wanted to stay in the frayed chaos of life, we would have no need of heaven. We live our busy lives in chaos because we are searching for the solution to our restless-ness. Jesus is the only answer.

Heaven is the place that we thirst for. Beach days suggest the beauty, wholeness, and adventure we will experience for eternity in God's presence. God is preparing a place for each of us where every longing and desire will be satisfied.

Jesus is preparing our place in heaven.

Hair-Dryer Prayers

The LORD . . . delights in the prayers of the upright.
                                    Proverbs 15:8

A woman's life has many busy seasons. Sometimes, finding time to sit down and eat is hard, much less offer a formal prayer. In college, I had a roommate who prayed as she dried her hair in the morning. She said that it was a reliable, undistracted time when she could connect with God.

I don't think God has a preference as to when or how we connect with him in prayer. He delights in a sincere heart that offers him daily concerns and thanks. Prayer time connects us with God so that we can listen for his whisper of love. If that can happen under the hair dryer, it can happen anywhere!

Be creative. Pray for your loved ones as you iron their clothes. Pray for God's joy in your day as you apply makeup in the morning. Pray for the world's health and well-being when you are stuck in traffic. God hears all of our prayers.

God's help and comfort are available 24/7. God asks us to seek him, and he tells us that he will respond if we reach out to him. Make time for that today.

Connect with God in prayer!

Warm Meals with Warm Hugs

Encourage each other and build each other up.

1 Thessalonians 5:11

In times of transition or crisis, many church families reach out to others, providing warm meals and warm hugs. A home-cooked meal and a smile of encouragement can be the quickest route to meeting the heart's need.

Just as a long-distance runner needs extra encouragement to get past the aching legs to the finish line, we all wear down and gasp for an encouraging push through the slumps in our own lives. Paul urged the Thessalonians to encourage each other, knowing that we need the constant support of family and friends to be at our best.

Open your eyes to those in your life who may need an extra word of encouragement, a hot meal, a thoughtful card, or a warm hug to brighten their day. By giving of yourself for the encouragement of another, you will also be strengthened. Think of people who have encouraged you in your race by offering love and support and by cheering you on. Take a moment to say thank you with a note, an e-mail, or flowers. When we show appreciation to others, our lives flourish.

Encourage someone today!

Megaphone Silence

After the wind there was an earthquake, but the LORD
was not in the earthquake. And after the earthquake
there was a fire, but the LORD was not in the fire. And
after the fire there was the sound of a gentle whisper.

1 Kings 19:11-12

A million things compete for our attention. To listen and
really hear, we need to swim out of the world's noisy ocean
and take a quiet moment on the sand.

Our all-powerful God does not choose to shout in an
earthquake, a fire, or the wind. He does not demand our
attention above the roar of life. God waits until he has our
attention and comes alongside when we are still enough to
hear his gentle whisper.

To hear God's voice, we need to quiet our hearts. God
delights in speaking with a heart humble enough to be still
and listen to him.

We hear God's gentle whispers of love in the beauty of
creation. Soft puffy clouds glide through a blue sea of sky,
children spill across the backyard, a friend offers a listening
ear, the family laughs together, and the sun rises on a brand
new day.

God speaks his love all around us; to perceive it, we
must listen.

Listen to God's gentle whisper.

Come Alive!

Jesus told him, "I am the way, the truth, and the life. No one can come to the Father except through me."

John 14:6

Just as the distance from our world to the moon is too far for us to jump, the distance between us and God is too far to reach in our own power. Our sins keep us from our Creator. Our natural selfishness widens the gap between us and God.

When we turn from ourselves and admit that we need help, God points us to Jesus, who gave his life to bridge the gap that we cannot cross on our own. Jesus gave his life for ours so that we may live!

Jesus shows us the way to a joy-filled life. When we admit our need and turn from our old ways, we can walk through life with faith and love. Walk in Jesus' way and experience the richness of a joy-filled life!

Jesus is the only way to God and the answer to all our searching. From this day forward, personally believe in the work that Christ did on your behalf on the cross. Grow in relationship with Jesus. He wants to be your Savior and friend, now and forever.

Trust wholly in Jesus.

The Burden of Baggage

Jesus said, "Come to me, all of you who are weary and carry heavy burdens, and I will give you rest."

Matthew 11:28

We women stuff things into our bags—makeup, car keys, diapers, umbrellas, cell phones, planners, food, drinks . . . everything. We do the same with our emotional baggage. We pack bags with worry, anger, frustration, disappointment, and pain. Sometimes we become emotional pack rats—we're so used to our emotional baggage that it becomes a comfort.

We stuff our days with last week's disappointing news and yesterday's squabble with our neighbor. We drag along our past regrets and failures. We haul overstuffed bags of guilt around with us, day in and day out.

Jesus wants to take our baggage from us and turn it over to God.

God wants the fullest life for us. Life isn't nearly as enjoyable and vibrant when we are sore and cramped from hauling our emotional baggage. Jesus offers us rest and emotional healing in exchange for the load. He will handle each of our burdens with loving care.

Turn your baggage over to Jesus and receive his healing and rest.

Give your baggage to God!

Beautiful in Time

God has made everything beautiful for its own time.
Ecclesiastes 3:11

Have you ever set your heart on something and been completely disappointed when your hopes didn't work out? In most of our lives, disappointments come in large and small sizes every day. The trashman comes early, the car wash isn't open, and the weather is lousy when we counted on sunshine. The test results come back positive, the kids perform poorly, and loved ones let us down. Life often falls short of our expectations.

How we handle the unexpected reflects our deepest attitudes. We may close up and shut life out, become depressed, or feel angry. It is easy to be dissatisfied and frustrated when things haven't gone our way.

If we realize that the way things are going is for the best—that they will become beautiful in God's time, not ours—then we can let the disappointments go.

The things we hope for don't always come through in the way that we expect, but there is still something to be enjoyed. Even in disappointment, there is joy.

The joys of each day are fleeting, so we must treasure them before they disappear. We have to release our disappointments to discover the joys.

Treasure today's joy and beauty.

Kitchen Cleanup

She carefully watches everything in her household and suffers nothing from laziness. Proverbs 31:27

Life gets overwhelming sometimes. Toys, dust bunnies, cobwebs, and heaps of junk mail soon clutter our kitchens when we're not organized. We need a strategy for clearing clutter and making room for the important things in life.

Mail always gets out of control when it isn't tackled immediately. It takes about ten minutes of undivided attention and discipline to sort out the pile. Then the usual papers that come home from school, church, and work end up in another stack on the kitchen counter. Another ten minutes per day takes care of most of it. Write down what is important and trash the rest.

Where to write the important things? A hallway collection of wall organizers can help tremendously: one for mail and keys, a bulletin board for hanging the calendar and invitations, and a write-and-wipe board for the weekly schedule.

Life gets complicated and messy on busy days in busy families. God does not want us to be overwhelmed. He wants us to have an orderly life that makes room for things that really matter. Take time each day to tidy up and create a welcoming home for your heart.

Make space for what is most important.

Tale of Two Plates

She dresses in fine linen and purple gowns. . . . She is clothed with strength and dignity.　　Proverbs 31:22, 25

Imagine two different plates. One plate has been carefully washed, and though it is not new, it shines with simple beauty. The second plate has not been cleaned lately, and though it is new, it looks dull and lifeless. Home-baked chocolate chip cookies, still warm and fresh from the oven, are arranged on each plate. If you had the choice, which plate would you take your cookie from?

On many days, it is hard to manage an attractive appearance. It is much easier to pull on sweatpants and baggy sweatshirts. But in the same way that we would choose a cookie from the well-kept plate, human nature gravitates toward a well-groomed appearance.

In our society, physical appearance counts a great deal. Physical appearance is not a waste of time, as a well-cared-for exterior is important in winning the attention of our physically oriented society. To be effective in sharing God's love with the world, we don't want our exterior appearance to obscure the simple beauty of his love shining from within.

Take care of yourself and be at your very best today.

A welcoming exterior invites others.

Hunger and Thirst

Jesus replied, "Anyone who drinks this water will soon become thirsty again. But those who drink the water I give will never be thirsty again. It becomes a fresh, bubbling spring within them, giving them eternal life."

John 4:13-14

I love to cook meals that take longer than six hours to make. My old friend the Crock-Pot, filled with simmering garlic, Italian dressing, and a pot roast, makes an irresistible dinner. As it cooks all day, hunger also builds, and snacking to suppress the hunger doesn't satisfy. It remains until we eat the pot roast, the source of the wonderful Crock-Pot aroma.

We humans are born to be dissatisfied . . . until we identify the source of our need. We can search our whole lives for something to fulfill our longings, but we often don't know what we're looking for. Different days bring different ways of attempting to satisfy the thirst—shopping, church activities, relationships. Our culture encourages indulgence in more money, success, and power. But the satisfactions of having more things, perfectly controlled relationships, a position on the church board, or a completely filled schedule are only temporary.

Jesus created our thirst, and only he can satisfy it.

Jesus satisfies our longings.

Broken Arm

The LORD hears his people when they call to him for help. He rescues them from all their troubles.

Psalm 34:17

One night after dinner, our oldest son fell from the monkey bars while playing in our backyard with his brothers. His fall initiated a grueling string of events: rushing to the hospital, struggling through X-rays, and enduring a two-hour emergency surgery for a severe break through his elbow. Life changed in an instant.

Life often brings suffering. It is tough to deal with the unexpected pains of life, and as we endure, we cry for help.

As parents, it is hard to see our children suffer. It must also be tough for God to see us, his children, living through pain. We are fragile, but he is powerful. When we feel that we cannot endure, he strengthens us.

The Lord hears us when we call on his name. Our Lord God knows our pain, grief, and sorrows, and he promises to rescue us in his time. God is as close as the air we breathe.

Recognize God's presence in everything you do. Call out to him, and he will draw near. Ask him for help, and know that he is with you. God's presence will bring you peace.

Take courage in God's presence.

Intentional Thankfulness

Be thankful in all circumstances, for this is God's will for you who belong to Christ Jesus.   1 Thessalonians 5:18

Every single day, we are faced with a choice. We can see the things we have to be thankful for, or we can focus on what we don't have and say, "Poor me!"

It is so easy to fall into the self-pity trap. Discontent can arise over anything—the big house we don't have, the nicer vehicle, better figure, longer vacation, better job, or more attentive loved ones—when we compare our lives with others'.

Instead of a pity party, God wants us to experience thankfulness in all circumstances. *All circumstances!* That means that even when we think we need something more, we must practice being thankful for what we already have.

Each day is a gift! Break free of the self-pity trap. Concentrate on what you have been given rather than on what you don't have. Make this a great day by counting your blessings. You will receive the incredibly fulfilling gift of joy!

Then take your real needs to the Lord, who promises to provide everything we need.

Choose to give thanks.

Healing for the Heart

Whatever their sickness or disease, or if they were demon possessed or epileptic or paralyzed—he healed them all.   Matthew 4:24

Broken bones and other ailments hold many lessons for us. However much our bodies come apart, physicians can begin the healing process by putting the pieces back in the right places. With broken bones, there is nothing that we can do to heal after that except to wait and pray. Healing is a mystery.

So many things in life bring brokenness. Relationships crumble, jobs fall apart, homes and possessions fade away—yet there is hope. Jesus offers us healing for our brokenness, and he mends our heartaches as well as our physical pain. To experience his healing, we must simply come to Jesus.

The healing process for bones begins with putting the broken pieces back in the proper places. The healing process for every life ailment begins with putting our broken pieces back in God's hands. We don't know how to handle the remnants of our messes, but Jesus heals them by his power.

Matthew said that Jesus "healed them all," and Jesus will heal us. We can be made whole again by trusting in his healing power.

Jesus is the great physician.

Creative Juices

*Put on your new nature, and be renewed as you learn
to know your Creator and become like him.*

Colossians 3:10

Children were made for creating . . . and so are adults.
Adults often shortchange themselves and their children
of the necessary time and materials for discovery through
creativity.

Whether it be a multicolored Play-Doh sculpture, a
sand tower, a bucket of mud and berry soup, or a toy-truck
road in the dirt by the back door, children are always creating something. One famous artist said that every child is
born an artist. The world's criticism must take away our
courage to create somewhere along the road to adulthood.

As Colossians says, we are to put on our new selves, get
to know our Creator, and become more like him each day.
A great way to grow in knowing God is to imitate him by
taking courage and learning to create again.

Creative opportunities are endless. Reflect on what brings
you the most joy, then make a commitment to yourself to
slow down and spend time creating. It begins with something as simple as making a delicious meal, cross-stitching a
wall hanging, or planting a spring flower container. Discover
your creative roots and get to know your Creator.

God gives us our creativity.

Sharpen Up!

*Using a dull ax requires great strength, so sharpen
the blade.*   Ecclesiastes 10:10

Have you ever tried to slice an apple with a very dull knife
or tried to take a great photograph with a disposable camera?
Have you ever tried to operate a computer program with no
prior experience or write a handwritten note with a crayon?

It is hard to perform many simple tasks with inadequate
tools. Doing things without the proper training or tools is
like chopping wood with a dull ax. The job can be done,
but it is frustrating, and the results are disappointing.

God wants our lives to be effective. He gave us skills,
knowledge, and creativity to share with others . . . and he
wants us to be successful in reaching our world for him.

Don't feel guilty about investing in yourself. We all need
sharpened skills and tools to live effectively. Time spent
in sharpening the saw will make your work easier and free
your mind of frustrations.

A fully enabled life is effective for God and his work.
Your light will shine and you will be filled with joy. Make
time today to refurbish your tools, invest in yourself, and
sharpen your skills.

Sharpen your tools!

The Refuge of Home

Cheerfully share your home with those who need a meal or a place to stay.   1 Peter 4:9

Home is a welcome refuge amid the chaos of life. Coming home after a time away brings a fresh surge of energy and comfort. It is unspeakably wonderful to have a place where everyone who enters its doors is accepted and loved for who they are.

It is important to decorate and arrange a dwelling place to suit individual tastes, for familiarity and love transform a house into a home. Like a balloon that loses air in the hot sun, we also run out of steam over time. I like to think of home as a place to reinflate the soul. We all need a place to recharge our batteries, refuel our emotional tank, refresh our exterior, and revive our spirit.

Cheerfully sharing the comforts of home with those who have no such place is an important way to serve others. When the world takes its toll through rejection, criticism, failure, and heartbreak, we all need someplace to fall back on while we regain perspective and catch our breath.

Make your home a refuge of acceptance, love, and joy!

Home is for renewal and sharing.

Leaving the Details to God

God will generously provide all you need. Then you will always have everything you need and plenty left over to share with others. 2 Corinthians 9:8

"What do I want to do when I grow up?" The answer is usually lived out in a mixture of practicality and dreams. Like a teacher with a passion for learning and the nurse who loves caring for others, doing what we were made to do brings much peace and satisfaction.

To get there, we need to notice how God is drawing our hearts, move in that direction, and leave the details up to him.

The shout of doubt is usually louder than the whisper of invitation. As we discover what we want to do, we are dragged down by practicality. God wants us to listen to our dreams and follow them, leaving the unknowns in his hands. Time, money, open doors, right relationships, and resources are part of what God loves to provide in making our dreams possible.

When God calls you toward something bigger than you could plan for yourself, know that he will lavishly provide for your needs. "God doesn't call the equipped; he equips the called!"

Go, and leave the details to God!

God abundantly meets your needs.

Coming Clean

Elisha sent a messenger out to him with this message:
"Go and wash yourself seven times in the Jordan River."
2 Kings 5:10

Naaman, a powerful warrior, was favored by his king,
but he suffered from leprosy, a terrible skin disease. To
be healed, Naaman followed a friend's advice and visited
God's prophet Elisha. When Naaman arrived, Elisha didn't
even greet him personally, but sent him a message to bathe
seven times in the Jordan River. Naaman was annoyed.
Why should he bathe in a muddy river? Why seven times?
After he had traveled all this way, couldn't Elisha have met
him personally?

It was hard for Naaman to overcome his pride and
follow a treatment that seemed too easy to work, but he
followed Elisha's instructions, and he was healed.

The cure for our sin also seems too easy to work. Just
believing that Jesus died to pay for our sins doesn't seem
powerful enough.

Take the first step into the muddy river of faith and
begin to heal your soul. We don't understand why steps of
faith allow us to come clean, but we are assured of eternal
life simply through believing in Jesus.

Take the first step toward healing. Believe in Jesus today!

Have faith and come clean!

Simply More Joy

*Seek the Kingdom of God above all else, and live
righteously, and he will give you everything you need.*
Matthew 6:33

Not long ago, our aged computer went kaput. Its old box-style monitor took up a huge portion of our desk, so it felt great to reclaim that space for a sleeker, more modern one. What a wonderful feeling to enjoy something simpler!

Sometimes we feel overwhelmed when our lives are cluttered with too many commitments. Freeing up space on our calendars often helps alleviate time-crunched stress by limiting certain activities to make room for more important things.

God says that making room for him first in our lives and allowing the rest to fall into place will give us freedom. When we prioritize our activities by putting God first, we are able to experience the joy, love, and life found in simpler things. Putting God first happens best when we talk with God and open our lives to his guidance and strength for clearing the clutter.

Make room today for the most important things. Put God first and all your other priorities will fall into place. A simple life brings much joy.

Put God first.

Content with What We Have

It is a good thing to receive wealth from God and the good health to enjoy it. To enjoy your work and accept your lot in life—this is indeed a gift from God.

Ecclesiastes 5:19

It is hard to be content in a world saturated with advertisements claiming that happiness comes from having more. Our world endorses more clothes, more cars, more things. Our lives revolve around bigger and better, and our culture promotes younger skin, youthful looks, and young bodies.

It is easy to feel dissatisfied, because looks fade, skin sags, clothes wear out, and hair grays. Money comes and money goes, and bigger cannot always be bought, except as a bigger credit card bill.

It is hard not to want superficial things, but God's logic defies that of our culture. The Bible says that contentment is a gift from God, and a fulfilled life comes from contentment!

Imagine how our lives would change if we chose to be content rather than investing in more, bigger, better, and younger. When we choose thankfulness for what we already have, we become free to enjoy it!

Today is a precious gift from God. Pursue contentment and enjoy each day!

Be content with what you have.

Taking the Long Way

*This is what the L*ORD *says: "Stop at the crossroads and look around. Ask for the old, godly way, and walk in it. Travel its path, and you will find rest for your souls."*

Jeremiah 6:16

If your part of the country is like ours, you travel new highways built to bypass scenic old byways. By traveling in multiple lanes of traffic at breakneck speed, we miss the natural beauty found along country lanes. Flowering trees and wildflower meadows, rolling hills and fishing ponds bless our lives.

Slow down and experience life by savoring each moment, wherever you are. To rush by, surrounded by concrete and multilane traffic, is to miss the ride altogether, adding stress instead of beauty to the time we are given.

In a culture obsessed with life in the fast lane, it is hard to be more intentional. We must each decide at the crossroads what type of experience we want in our lives. Deciding to experience more peace and joy in life by slowing down and enjoying the ride takes courage. However, stepping out of the fast lane even for a moment brings peace, beauty, and joy to each day.

Choose to slow down and experience the joy of life's natural beauty!

Slow down and enjoy the ride!

Giving Up Chocolate

I know it is important to love him with all my heart and all my understanding and all my strength, and to love my neighbor as myself. This is more important than to offer all of the burnt offerings and sacrifices required in the law.
Mark 12:33

Around this time of year, it is common to hear people mention what they are giving up for Lent. Many give up chocolate or other desserts. Taking time off from fatty foods may be good for the diet, but deprivation of life's pleasures may not be what God is looking for.

Lent is a time of preparation for celebrating Christ's death and resurrection at Easter. Just as many celebrate Mardi Gras as the last hoorah before Lent, many believe that God wants them to give up something they enjoy to remember Jesus' sacrifice before Easter.

God is more concerned with the condition of our hearts than with an outward show of obedience and sacrifice. We have to examine our motives. Are we performing out of love for God or to get recognition and approval?

God knows what is in our hearts. He loves it when we show our love for him by doing his work. Clear out your heart to make room for a loving attitude.

Examine your heart.

Daffodil Dressing

If God cares so wonderfully for wildflowers that are here today and thrown into the fire tomorrow, he will certainly care for you. Why do you have so little faith?

Matthew 6:30

Everywhere we look, we see signs of new life. Soon winter will be past and nature will awaken to shout its beauty to the warming world.

Each year, just as my hopes are set on colorful daffodil blooms, a deep freeze settles in overnight and the daffodils are left frosty and lifeless. Every year I worry and wonder, *Are they dead? Will they come back?* Yet, the next sunny day, I'm relieved to see the daffodils standing tall again.

Just as daffodils can count on their fancy yellow spring apparel, we can count on our Creator to meet our every need. Jesus cares much more for us than for the beautiful spring flowers that last only a few days. We are precious to him; we do not need to worry about the things we need, because God delights in caring for us.

When life leaves us empty and hopeless, we can trust the God who looks after each beautiful flower to care for our needs.

God cares for us.

A Hearty Welcome

May the Lord make your love for one another and for all people grow and overflow, just as our love for you overflows. 1 Thessalonians 3:12

"Jenniferrrrrrr!" I heard it from across the crowded room. As I turned my head, I could see outstretched arms and a great big smile. What a welcome sight in such an unfamiliar crowd! A familiar face with a giant greeting of love is what we sometimes need to feel at home.

In today's world, we are so disconnected from human touch by busyness and electronics that overflowing love and hearty welcomes are needed more than ever. Skip the halfhearted but less risky wave to a friend when you meet. Smile big and show her that you're happy to see her!

God loves it when we love one another. Love comes from God, and when we live in love, we live more courageously and give more generously of ourselves to others. Pray that today God will pour his love into your life and enable that same love to overflow to the people around you.

Go ahead—greet your family with a hearty "Good morning!" and a kiss. Let God's love flow from your heart into the lives of others.

God is our source of love.

Pet Store Freedom

God, with undeserved kindness, declares that we are righteous. He did this through Christ Jesus when he freed us from the penalty for our sins. Romans 3:24

One memorable day while our family was browsing the aisles of the local pet store, we encountered the bird section. Usually, someone begs to buy one and bring it home, but this day, our oldest son wanted to help the colorful winged wonders by buying them all and setting them free. Perhaps at the ripe old age of six, he understood that being caged is torture—we all need to fly free.

God made the human spirit, like the birds, to be free. Our hearts soar when they are free to grow, to breathe. Yet out of fear, we have a hard time freeing ourselves and others by releasing our grasp instead of trying to control.

It is easy to make rules and restrictions for others. We see ourselves as superior, and we think that everyone needs to be like us in order to measure up. When we feel this way, we need to reflect on our own imperfections and God's acceptance of us as we are. Today, free yourself to accept others for who they are.

Jesus loves us as we are!

Saint Patrick's Day

He will teach us his ways, and we will walk in his paths.
                                                    Isaiah 2:3

Saint Patrick is best remembered for preaching throughout Ireland. Listen to part of Saint Patrick's beautiful prayer for God's protection and Christ's presence:

> As I arise today, may the strength of God pilot me,
> the power of God uphold me,
> the wisdom of God guide me.
> May the eye of God look before me,
> the ear of God hear me,
> the word of God speak for me.
> May the hand of God protect me,
> the way of God lie before me,
> the shield of God defend me,
> the host of God save me. . . .
> Christ when I sit,
> Christ when I stand,
> Christ in the heart of everyone who thinks of me,
> Christ in the mouth of everyone who speaks of me,
> Christ in every eye that sees me,
> Christ in every ear that hears me. Amen.

Prayer influences our world!

Bubbling Brownies

Christ offered himself to God as a perfect sacrifice for our sins.   Hebrews 9:14

At our house, we like to make dinners special when we are all together. One memorable night, I made brownies and, like every busy woman, multitasked at the same time. Usually, watching the boys, talking on the phone, and stirring brownies isn't a problem. That night, I must have missed an ingredient—the brownies came out bubbling.

Jesus offered himself as the perfect sacrifice for our sins. His death on the cross was not missing a single ingredient. All we need to do is to accept Jesus' perfect sacrifice for our sins and imperfections. His complete love covers our inadequacies. Though we make mistakes, hurt others' feelings, bounce checks, and have accidents, Christ offers us hope by covering our imperfections.

Although we are imperfect in everything we do (including brownies), when we accept Jesus' death on the cross to cover what we lack, we are made whole and perfect in God's eyes. In Christ, we are accepted as blameless and perfect and can have eternal life with him in heaven forever. We have a sure hope despite our imperfections!

Jesus gives us hope for the future!

The Gas Gauge

It is useless for you to work so hard from early morning until late at night, anxiously working for food to eat; for God gives rest to his loved ones.   Psalm 127:2

So often in our lives, we drive here and there, near and far, to accomplish our to-do lists. With gas prices so high, it is prudent to drive with one eye on the gas gauge and one eye on the road, trying to refuel as seldom as possible.

Many lives resemble a car's empty gas tank. We drive ourselves to do more and go farther until eventually we even run out of fumes to travel on. As women, we do so much, but when we don't take time to refuel our souls, we run out of gas. Knowing our need for downtime, God hopes that we'll plan for times of rest.

This week, take Sunday to recharge with the family. Make time for weekly refueling by doing something that makes your heart sing, like scrapbooking or going out for coffee with a friend. Make a daily routine of refueling from God's Word, the ultimate refreshment. Take time to rest today!

Regularly refuel your soul.

Shine Your Light

You are the light of the world—like a city on a hilltop that cannot be hidden.   Matthew 5:14

Once, while camping at a primitive site in the Rocky Mountains, I was thankful for a light—a flashlight, that is. On a starless overcast night, it is easy to get lost. Thankfully, with the flashlight, we made it safely back to camp.

Without a light, we are all lost, without direction in the starless night of life. Jesus talks about his light in Matthew 5:16: "In the same way, let your good deeds shine out for all to see, so that everyone will praise your heavenly Father." Sharing the light is a primary reason for living.

Practically speaking, light shines most effectively through joyful lives. True, lasting joy comes from the hope and peace found in a rich relationship with Jesus. Joy radiates from a sincere heart and illuminates our surrounding world, often with no words spoken.

Set your sights on God and his light. Share the light you have with others. You are the light of the world. Go and live joyfully, and shine your light for him today!

Shine with God's love and joy.

First Day of Spring

Ask the LORD for rain in the spring, for he makes the storm clouds. And he will send showers of rain so every field becomes a lush pasture. Zechariah 10:1

Oh! What beauty and color bloom in springtime! The miraculous brown forsythia twigs burst into yellow flowers, usually the first blossoms of spring. The greening leaves unfold into the sun and the perfume of the flowering trees and lilacs wafts in the breeze. It is as if all of creation has been holding its breath and can now begin to breathe again. The birds busy themselves making nests, the half-warmed cabbage-white butterflies taste the first blooming nectar, and rich greens return to the faded brown landscape.

In the returning glory of spring, we are reminded of Jesus' death at Easter. Each new burst of flower seems to say, "We've overcome winter's death and returned to full life!" All creation rejoices in spring with Christ's resurrection.

God brings life back to the earth; his care is never-ending. He waters the earth and breathes warmth to thaw the frozen ground.

Just as God revives the springtime world, he can awaken new life in you. Allow the beauty of spring and God's creation to speak to your heart this season.

God brings the earth to life!

Living Love

Three things will last forever—faith, hope, and love—and the greatest of these is love.   1 Corinthians 13:13

It is interesting to walk about the house after it has emptied in the morning. Clothes are strewn, beds unmade, coffee still warming, dirty dishes on the table. It would be easy to resent the untidiness and disorder, but life is made for more than hard feelings. Next time, I can ask for help before everyone is running for the day.

Even when socks are strewn on the floor, dinner gets cold, plans are set aside, and hopes go unfulfilled, love unconditionally. We never quite get our own act together, so why would we expect a perfect performance from everyone else?

God's love withstands tough times and misunderstandings. Love loves no matter what, saying, "You don't have to do anything to make me love you more. I love you because you're you."

When we discover our faith and believe in Jesus' life and message, we find that hope is the attitude that brings life to life! Love is a combination of hope and faith; we love because God first loved us.

Give the world around you the gift that lasts forever. Choose to love others through the tough stuff today!

Live God's love today!

Names for Each Rose

Look up into the heavens. Who created all the stars? He brings them out like an army, one after another, calling each by its name. Because of his great power and incomparable strength, not a single one is missing.

Isaiah 40:26

Each spring about this time, a few new roses arrive in the mail. Specially ordered, they come bare-root, meaning that they are dormant and look like thorny brown sticks. It is hard to tell them apart, so each rose is marked with a label. Each rose will have a different height, color, and needs, so each planting location is based on the rose's label. Without its label, even a rose is lost.

Isaiah 40 tells us of God's care for each part of creation. The Creator of heaven and earth knows every particle. Even the stars, infinite in number and appearing quite similar to our naked eyes, have special names. Not one atom of God's creation is lost; each bit has its own value.

God has specially created each one of us. Not one of us has been left outside of his loving, watchful care. God hopes that we will grow and bloom into lives full of beauty.

God knows us each by name.

No Grass beneath the Swings

Accept each other just as Christ has accepted you so that God will be given glory.   Romans 15:7

Life is full of struggles. People make rude comments when one is dealing with a disobedient child in public; grades are poor despite hard study and good effort; the rejection letter comes for yet another hoped-for position; the baby seen by ultrasound is motionless; the pink slip is on the desk. Sometimes life just takes our breath away. We all need someone to fall back on, a place of acceptance to return to while catching our breath.

Imagine a place that everyone wants to come home to, where everyone is accepted just as they are. In such a home, rest is easy, food is hearty, and laughter is rich. It has a backyard for messy popsicles in which the grass is worn away under the swings. "I love you" and "I'm proud of you" are frequently heard in conversation.

Home is a place for the weary to rest and for broken hearts to heal. Together, we can share gratitude for blessings and pray about burdens. Love and acceptance are essential for riding out life's storms.

Make your home a place of acceptance—a place for each heart to be at rest.

Make your home a loving shelter.

A Handful of Spring

Look, the winter is past, and the rains are over and gone. The flowers are springing up, the season of singing birds has come, and the cooing of turtledoves fills the air.   Song of Songs 2:11-12

The rains may not be over, but winter is surely past and flowers are springing up. Where we live, the loveliest sight this time of year is the daffodils. Their bright yellow petticoats bring fresh sunshine to dreary days.

I love spring flowers, but I easily become too busy to enjoy them. It is easy to back out of the garage on a single-minded errand and forget to even glimpse at nature's beauty. It is much easier to keep running than to take time to enjoy the flowers and thank God, who created them.

God has placed so much beauty in our lives. Each flower is fleeting, but God created it just for you! He wants to speak his love to you in the vibrant yellow of daffodils against the cloudless blue sky.

God hopes that you will recognize his tender care in the delicate spring blooms washed by gentle rains. Take a few moments to gather a bouquet of daffodils—springtime by the handful—and know that they were made just for you!

Enjoy God's beautiful creation.

Stormy Search for Meaning

O God, you are my God; I earnestly search for you. My soul thirsts for you; my whole body longs for you in this parched and weary land where there is no water.

Psalm 63:1

March supposedly comes in like a lion and goes out like a lamb. With howling wind, thunder and lightning, pelting rain, and hail, the stormy part of March often matches our inner struggles. Our interiors can also storm and rage.

As humans, we were born to be dissatisfied without Jesus' love in our hearts. Our culture supports buying more possessions and putting more items on the calendar as ways to fill the restless longing. When we increase our status and make ourselves needed, popular, and important, the internal storm seems momentarily quieted. Yet gaining all the recognition on earth will never stop the anxious ache of our need to be known.

All things on earth fade away—our bodies, our fame, our power and recognition. The only security on which to build our lives is Jesus.

Only in living for someone beyond ourselves does life have meaning. Only Jesus can calm the storm of our search for significance. Seek inner peace by living in relationship with him.

Jesus answers life's search for meaning.

Spread a Little Beauty

If you have a gift for showing kindness to others, do it gladly.   Romans 12:8

I go out of my way to drive through a nearby town when I'm doing errands. All of the town's regular streets have been made into boulevards planted with flowers, shrubs, and trees that are regularly groomed. As I pass by their miles of flowering gardens, I think that this must be part of our reason for existing. Heavy traffic passes by these beautiful gardens in just the course of the day. How much richer and more beautiful our existence is with such oases!

It is hard to squeeze a few dollars out of the monthly budget to spend on flowers. We can "cheapskate" away from beauty, but what is life if not a chance to make the world more beautiful?

Start with a little pot of pansies for springtime—their colorful smiles will cheer you up. Go ahead! Spend a little of yourself to show kindness to others today.

Brighten your world by adding a few beautiful flowers to your daily routine. Kindness and beauty cost a little, but their day-brightening benefits change the world.

Share kindness and beauty!

The High Price of Ambition

Remember the LORD your God. He is the one who gives you power to be successful.　　　Deuteronomy 8:18

Ambition is a common sign of our times. Jobs, cars, and houses are frequently upgraded, and this comes at a high price.

As our lives speed up and free time dwindles, we need to ask, "What is motivating me to do this?" When the underlying answer is "to be more important, to have a bigger house, to get a higher status, to earn a bigger name for myself," take an inventory of what really matters in your life. Will those people you're seeking to impress be caring for you in thirty years? Are you sacrificing enjoyable family time to get ahead?

Balance is needed in all things, so seek out what is really important in your life. Since God rules over all things, he alone gives each of us the ability to be successful. If he is able to give us all that we need, we can relax and trust him wholeheartedly.

We don't have to be overly ambitious and busy. God watches over us, and he will not let us fall. Focus on building meaningful relationships with your family, friends, and Jesus.

Jesus holds our lives in his hands.

Gaining More

Come, let's build a great city for ourselves with a tower that reaches into the sky. This will make us famous and keep us from being scattered all over the world.

Genesis 11:4

It is natural to want to impress others with our credentials, but when we elevate ourselves, others get pushed down and we miss out on simpler, more worthwhile human connections. Such striving leaves only loneliness.

The people of Babel decided to make a name for themselves and create their own glory. God saw their hearts and frustrated their efforts because their goal was to build a monument to themselves so that they wouldn't need God.

It's easy for us to get wrapped up in plans for self-advancement. We allow our achievements to define our identity and self-worth, and thus replace God. In serving others, we gain much more than fame. When we are not wrapped up in ourselves, we can attend to the simpler things that make life significant.

God helps us to be who we hope to be—women secure enough in God's love to pass this love along to others. Trust God to lift you up in his time.

God is our hope.

Silk Iris

O Lord my God, you have performed many wonders for us. Your plans for us are too numerous to list. You have no equal. Psalm 40:5

All winter, an arrangement of silk Dutch irises, rich indigo with contrasting yellow, brightened our flower-deprived eyes. Yet the fake flowers in this arrangement cannot compare with the beauty of real flowers just beginning to bloom. What I thought was so beautiful looks phony next to the real thing.

Similarly, our real selves are much more beautiful than the masks we wear throughout life. To please others, we put on an appearance that we think they will like. To be accepted, we try to be the smartest, prettiest, and most athletic woman. However, the artificial version of ourselves can never measure up to the God-given beauty of the real thing.

In his infinite goodness, God has made each of us to shine in a unique way. Pleasing others is a culturally acceptable goal, but it disappoints God when we are not true to ourselves. Unless we are being real, and growing each day to be more like Jesus, we are not beautiful in the way that God planned. God created us with dreams, gifts, and talents. Discover yourself today—the real, beautiful you.

God has big plans for our lives.

Sure As the Sun Rises

Faith is the confidence that what we hope for will actually happen; it gives us assurance about things we cannot see. Hebrews 11:1

With twilight colors changing, beach sunsets reveal the miraculous touch of God's hand. Brightly washed white sand bordered by turquoise water slowly dulls as the horizon brightens from yellow to orange and then to fiery magenta. The sun lowers itself into the water, stretching its shimmering reflections to touch those watching at water's edge.

The sunset changes our perspective, helping us to recognize a God much larger than ourselves. Each night as the sun leaves our view, we expect that it will return for the sunrise. At the most basic level, we exercise faith every day in trusting the sun to rise again.

Just as we trust our lives to the morning sun's return, we can entrust our whole lives to God. Though we cannot see him, or the sun, we have faith.

Jesus came to give his life for ours. Though we cannot see him, we know that he is here with us. Though we cannot physically feel his touch, our lives have Jesus' fingerprints all over them. Since Jesus rose again, we can hope for the sunrise even as the sun sets.

We are confident in Jesus' love.

April Fools

Even fools are thought wise when they keep silent; with their mouths shut, they seem intelligent.   Proverbs 17:28

April Fools may be a fun day, but playing the fool isn't usually a good idea. Years ago, when I was pregnant with our first child, I remember feeling quite vulnerable since I felt as big as a house. I will never forget two comments that I heard that year. One neighbor matter-of-factly stated that she knew we would have a boy because my behind was so large! Ouch! A well-meaning relative said loudly, "Well, how's the big momma doing?" I wanted to melt away into my maternity clothes.

As women, we have an amazing ability to speak before we think. Surely we all make comments that we don't really mean, and we try to catch the words on the way out. Open mouth, insert foot—the damage has already been done. Thoughtless words can be very hurtful.

Solomon writes that the fool's downfall is her mouth! Everyone knows a fool by the way she talks. Resolve to speak only after you've considered the other person's feelings. Put yourself in that person's shoes and speak words of life and encouragement. Bless the world with your words; ask Jesus to help you build others up.

Think before you speak.

Eagles' Wings

Those who trust in the LORD will find new strength. They will soar high on wings like eagles.   Isaiah 40:31

God had a good sense of humor when he created earth's animals. Some animals inspire wonder, such as the chameleon, with its ever-changing colors. We are amused by the antics of monkeys and chimpanzees, and the lion and the cheetah arouse awe. Eagles are able to soar effortlessly, far above the earth. I'm convinced that our souls were made to soar through the heavens and rise above it all.

In order to soar, we must be willing to spread our wings. It is difficult to take the risk, but we won't know how high we are able to fly until we try. The eagle does not soar by any effort of its own, but by riding the thermal currents. We can only soar when the Lord provides the lift under our wings.

Whether you are trying a new hobby, reconciling a rough relationship, or making some other new venture, put your trust in the Lord. He gives us wings to fly and loves to lift us up. His love will carry you higher than you dreamed possible!

Trust God for strength.

Pruning Time

I am the true grapevine, and my Father is the gardener. He cuts off every branch of mine that doesn't produce fruit, and he prunes the branches that do bear fruit so they will produce even more. John 15:1-2

Gardening is a favorite part of my life. I love to dig in the dirt, get my hands dirty, and plant a scene of beauty from materials that don't seem beautiful at all. For a garden to flourish, dead plant material has to be pruned in early spring.

Nearly every plant in our extensive gardens needs some sort of pruning. Each plant answers the question of how much to remove by its growth. In early April, new leaves and flower buds are forming and can easily be seen. The best pruning cuts off the dead matter where the growth stops so that the live part can keep growing, unhindered.

In John 15, Jesus talks about the master Gardener's pruning. God prunes off every bit of deadness in our lives so that we may continue to grow and reach our full potential. Though the pruning is never pleasant, the results in greater growth always make it worthwhile.

God guides our growth.

Rosy Rabbit Feast

Remain in me, and I will remain in you. For a branch cannot produce fruit if it is severed from the vine, and you cannot be fruitful unless you remain in me.

John 15:4

Every spring, we see signs of new life, including the bunnies in the garden. Though soft and fuzzy, with cute furry cotton-tails, rabbits always feast on the choicest garden plants. Just as Peter Rabbit always ate the best garden vegetables, our own backyard rabbits chew right through many branches on my favorite roses, leaving them severed and lifeless.

Jesus says that he is a vine and that we are the branches connected to him. If we stay connected to him through prayer, Scripture reading, and reflection, we will produce fruit in our lives.

The branches connected to the rose plant usually produce beautiful flowers. When the world comes along (like Peter Rabbit) and pulls us away from the life-giving plant, we are left useless, empty, and disconnected from Jesus, who gives us his life-giving power. We are severed from our vital source of life.

Stay connected to Jesus through time spent with him. Your rich life will reflect the quality of your relationship with him.

Remain connected with Jesus.

The Power Source

Yes, I am the vine; you are the branches. Those who remain in me, and I in them, will produce much fruit. For apart from me you can do nothing.   John 15:5

Consider the delicate balance in the following ordinary occurrences that affect our daily lives: Hurtling through space at an average speed of 18.4 miles per second, Earth is constantly changing its position with the sun. Not only is the earth orbiting around the sun, but it's also steadily rotating at 1,070 miles per hour. Each day, as Earth stays on her prescribed path, gravity continues to hold us to the ground, adequate fresh water exists, our hearts beat, our muscles move, our brains think, our cars continue down the road, we smile, and the sun shines. God has made all these miracles and sustains them, each moment of every day! We have countless reasons to thank God for holding all things in his divine balance. Apart from God, we really can do nothing.

Jesus says that when we stay connected to him in our daily lives, we will receive his power. Today, let the God who runs the universe and sustains each heartbeat connect with your life. Tap into the life that Jesus gives!

Let Jesus power your life.

Hand in Hand

If you remain in me and my words remain in you, you may ask for anything you want, and it will be granted!
John 15:7

As the mom of three young boys, I try not to do much shopping with them in tow. When we do go places, I hold their hands so that we stay together. If only God made moms with three arms . . .

Like a child holding his mother's hand against the push and pull of the crowd, we are connected to God against the push and pull of life. We cannot cause growth or bear fruit on our own. God only tells us to keep holding hands with him through life. He will guide us and lead us on to bigger dreams. Only we can decide to hold on and follow him.

If you've ever felt far from God (as we all have), the question is, "Who let go?" (it wasn't God). When that happens, call on him, for he promises to be near. God longs to give us the best things in life. Walk alongside him, holding his hand, and life will be full of love and laughter.

Keep holding God's hand!

Cute and Smart

When you produce much fruit, you are my true disciples.
This brings great glory to my Father.   John 15:8

Sometimes we find ourselves believing that in order to
make God happy, we must earn his love and acceptance.
After all, our culture encourages high performance if we
want to be accepted.

Through our lives, we learn that if we want to be loved,
we need to be cute (when we're kids), smart (when we're
in school), athletic and beautiful (when we're teenagers),
wealthy and busy (when we're adults), and hardworking
(at every stage of life) so that others will be happy with
our lives. When we're trained to do certain things for the
approval of others, we automatically assume that God
wants us to do these things too.

Jesus says only one thing will bring glory to God. That
one thing—to bear much fruit—has nothing to do with
our jumping through hoops.

Galatians 5:22-23 lists the fruit of the Spirit: "love, joy,
peace, patience, kindness, goodness, faithfulness, gentleness, and self-control." Jesus bears the fruit for us as we stay
connected to him. Let go of doing things for God and stay
close to him, for God accepts you as you are!

Remain close to God!

Runaway Bunny

*Let us come boldly to the throne of our gracious God.
There we will receive his mercy, and we will find grace
to help us when we need it most.*   Hebrews 4:16

For days now, our five-year-old has been trying to get near
the baby rabbit that lives in our yard. The young kit is
quite small and can usually be found feasting on the clover
just beyond the patio gardens. Every time Matthew sees the
baby bunny, he throws on his shoes and flies out the door.
Of course, when the door slams, the bunny runs. Matthew
walks through the plants in each garden, carefully searching
for his furry friend, but when approached, the little bunny
hops away.

Fortunately, when we approach God, he will not run
away. God will always be there, waiting for us to come. He
delights in our desire for him.

When we come to God in prayer, his eyes shine, and he
offers us a warm smile and welcoming arms. God knows us
and calls us each by name; he cares so much for us that he
even knows the number of hairs on our heads!

We can approach God's glorious throne with confidence.
God eagerly anticipates our call.

God wants us to approach him.

Dandelion Beauty

I don't mean to say that I have already achieved . . . perfection.
Philippians 3:12

Timepieces are essential for living according to a schedule. However, when a part breaks or the battery stops, our punctuality suffers.

Once, in such a watch-less predicament, I quickly bought a cheap replacement. For the first few weeks, the cheap watch appeared dependable and shined like new. But before long, the cheap finish wore off and the watch quit working as well. My cheap substitute did not wear well for long.

In life, we tend to think that others have their act more together than we do. We raise celebrities to an unrealistic level of prestige, which, like the cheap watch, doesn't last for long. The lives of our families, neighbors, and friends may appear beautiful on the outside, but on the inside, we all struggle with balancing our priorities, health, and relationships, and deciding who we will honor with our lives.

God tells us that no one is perfect except for himself, and filling our lives with cheap substitutes for his love will not provide lasting fulfillment. Today, see yourself and others through a more accurate lens. We all need a Savior's love.

Only Jesus is perfect.

April Showers

When the king smiles, there is life; his favor refreshes like a spring rain.   Proverbs 16:15

The beauty of spring flowers is dependent on spring rains. As their roots thaw and soak up moisture, the plants come alive; the rains are their source of life. I love to walk among the gardens after the rains. Water gently rolls down each petal and leaf, creating intricate designs; each flower caressed by gentle rain becomes more beautiful.

Like the spring flowers, our lives need rainy days for recharging. Rainy days sometimes spoil our plans, but they can help us slow down and reconnect with God, ourselves, and others.

Be intentional—call a friend and go out for lunch. Take a few moments to send a handwritten note. Read a favorite book or just enjoy a time of quiet. Take a walk through a garden or down a woodland path, and gaze upon the rain-washed beauty. Listen to the music of the rain. Smell the freshness that comes over the earth and allow the cool refreshment to soak into your soul.

Allow each rainy day to recharge your soul and make your life bloom more brightly and beautifully.

God's rainy days beautify our lives.

Dinner Tonight

I hold you by your right hand—I, the LORD your God. And I say to you, "Don't be afraid. I am here to help you."

Isaiah 41:13

"What's for supper?" is a standard kid question. Some nights, with little in the cupboards, we prepare something fresh and satisfying out of the few remaining ingredients— a miracle indeed! With anything but the mini-corn dogs in the corner of the freezer, tonight's dinner will be great!

We have every ingredient needed to make a great day—a little love, a sprinkle of smiles, a choice of joy, and patience instead of grouchiness. God's hand holds ours through everything that comes our way. We may feel as though there is nothing in our hearts that will make a great day, but when we call on Jesus, we have everything we need!

Many days won't go as we hope. Most of them won't follow our plan. When we turn our days over to our heavenly Father's care, we know that unexpected news, a longer-than-usual commute, a late arrival for a meeting, and all the unplanned glitches are part of his plan. When we are held in God's loving hands, there is no greater place to be. Make this a gourmet day!

Jesus supplies our needs!

Happy Meal Toys

Satisfy us each morning with your unfailing love, so we may sing for joy to the end of our lives. Psalm 90:14

The Golden Arches are quite an American fixture. Even two-year-olds can identify and name their favorite place to eat . . . McDonald's! Who wouldn't love a restaurant that sells famous fried foods complete with their very own toy? Cleverly, each toy comes with a list of the other toys that complete the collection. One toy is never enough.

Adults also live in a Happy Meal culture, wanting things we do not need and paying a high price to get them. We are so easily caught up in the frenzy to have more: a bigger house, bigger car, better riding mower, plusher vacation. However, those who "have it all" aren't satisfied either. What will satisfy us if having more things doesn't work?

In Psalm 90, Moses beautifully describes the only source of satisfaction. Only God can satisfy our restless hearts, and only he can answer our perpetual dissatisfaction. The secret to satisfaction is in asking the Source of all joy and peace each morning for his unending love. Filled with God's love, we are headed toward a lifetime of joy.

Let Jesus fulfill your life.

Feather by Feather

I will give you a new heart, and I will put a new spirit in you.
Ezekiel 36:26

Part of nature's miraculous spring awakening is the glorious transformation of the goldfinches. If you've ever seen goldfinches, you know how brilliant they are all summer, dressed in sunny yellow with their little black hats. Though goldfinches sing the same twittering sweet songs and fly the same lilting flight all year, they change appearance from their winter olive drab into summer's flashy garb feather by feather until June, when they shine in full glory.

When we live day by day in relationship with Jesus, we are gradually transformed into a new person who resembles Christ. Feather by feather, we lose our drab old self-centeredness. Our new lives become full of light through the power of Jesus.

How do we actually do that? Still not seeing a change? A good way to become more like Christ is to read the Bible, pray, and spend quiet times in reflection. Just as you spend time with loved ones to get to know and enjoy them, time spent with Christ will gradually bring about your new life in him. Day by day, feather by feather, you will shine with glorious new life.

Allow Christ to transform you.

Gordo's Return

While he was still a long way off, his father saw him coming. Filled with love and compassion, he ran to his son, embraced him, and kissed him.   Luke 15:20

April is the time of year to hang hummingbird feeders in our area. It is hard to believe that hummingbirds would return so early to the still-frosty Midwest, but this year, while I was washing breakfast dishes, a flash of red—a hummingbird hovering outside the window—caught my eye! On this fine frosty morning, I was overjoyed to see last year's hummer return! With a whoop of delight, I scrambled through cupboards to find the feeder, cooked the hummingbird nectar, and quickly hung it outdoors. Sure enough, my hummingbird friend Gordo was back, and I was delighted!

Luke describes the beautiful story of a son's return to his father. Though the son had left sometime before, the father always watched for his return. When he did come back, the father saw him from a long way off and ran to meet him with open arms.

Just as the father heartily welcomed the son and I greeted our favorite hummer Gordo, our heavenly Father delights in our company. He welcomes us with open arms!

God welcomes us with open arms.

Tax Time

We don't want to offend them, so go down to the lake and throw in a line. Open the mouth of the first fish you catch, and you will find a large silver coin. Take it and pay the tax for both of us.   Matthew 17:27

Each year around April 15, we have the privilege of paying our taxes. Some dread this time, and some are hopeful for a return on taxes already overpaid.

Jesus' disciples were questioned about whether or not Jesus would pay his Temple taxes. All Jewish males were required to pay these fees to the tax collectors. Peter answered that Jesus would pay the tax, and Jesus instructed Peter to go fishing for the money that was needed.

Though it is a bit unusual to go fishing for a valuable coin, Jesus provides for our needs however he wishes. Our job is to trust him and do what he tells us. Jesus did not magically present the needed coin, but required the disciples to do a little work and have a lot of faith.

Jesus wants to provide for our needs two thousand years later! He is willing and completely able to do this. We must do the work and have faith that Jesus will provide.

Jesus provides all that we need.

Busy Bees

Be still, and know that I am God!　　　　Psalm 46:10

Have you taken time today just to sit?

It is very hard for us women to unwind, relax, and fill back up. There is always something else to be done. One more load of laundry to do, one more dish to wash, one more phone call to make, one more diaper to change—something always needs our attention.

Today, consider leaving the list behind and finding a comfortable spot. Mine is out in the garden. The colors are soothing and the gentle breeze caressing, but it is still hard to let my mind unwind. The bees, I notice, have the same dilemma—they are busy going about their tasks and don't sit still for a moment.

In Psalm 46, God calls each of us to be still. Perhaps in the midst of our busyness, we forget that God is God and we are not. In the hustle and bustle, we may be wrapped in self-importance. God may know that by working so hard and moving so fast, we desperately need time to unwind, reflect, learn from our lives, and thank God for all that he is. Be still and know God today.

God calls us to rest.

Birds' Song of Praise

Shout joyful praises to God, all the earth! Sing about the glory of his name! Tell the world how glorious he is.

Psalm 66:1-2

This morning, we awakened to a symphony outside our open windows. The song sparrows whirred, the house finches twittered, the goldfinches added a squeaky-toy sound, and the bold cardinals belted out the lyrics—it was a reverie of sweet praise to the Waker of the sun.

God had such a sense of humor when he created the songbirds and their individual songs. As each offers up its praise, God must smile, for creation's praise pleases God.

If only we, too, awakened to each day with such exuberance and joy. Simply greeting our loved ones with a pleasant "Good morning" is often hard to do. If we recognized the day's potential for joy, we would greet each day with a smile. Just as each avian voice is endlessly lifted in praise to the Creator, so may our own voices resonate to our Lord in thanks for who he is and for his great love. It gives God much pleasure to hear our symphony of praise, as we love him with our hearts, voices, and lives.

God loves to hear our praise!

Living with Thorns

We can rejoice, too, when we run into problems and
trials, for we know that they help us develop endurance.
Romans 5:3

Today, while playing swords against the backyard bees, our
three-year-old took a nosedive into a rosebush. Yes, a nosedive. About ten oversized Band-Aids and many boo-boo
kisses later, he could hobble on. Life hurts sometimes.

God must have a sense of humor to place the world's
most beautiful flowers on thorn-laden stems. In life, we
encounter many experiences that mix prickles with beauty.
We encounter thorns in relationships, jobs, finances, and
church—for these aspects of life always have their pains.
The thorns also help us grow—and teach us to avoid a
scratchy encounter the next time.

Though thorns are painful, roses are beautiful, fragrant,
and healing. Life brings pain, and God heals us. When we
can see the roses past the thorns, we are one step closer to
healing our hurting hearts.

God hopes that when we encounter the thorns of life,
we will learn from them and be strengthened. Thankfulness,
even during pain, allows us to grow in character and find
joy. Allow God to heal your hurts and give you joy in life
today!

Let pain strengthen you.

Positive Influence

"Teacher," they said, "we know that you speak and teach what is right and are not influenced by what others think."
Luke 20:21

A brood of ducklings lived by a pond. One duckling just didn't fit in. Gray and awkward, the ugly duckling felt rejected because she looked different from the rest. As time passed, she realized through her reflection that she looked more like the nearby swans and less like an ugly duckling. She rested her value in the beautiful, elegant swan she was becoming and discovered her true beauty, which was not suppressed by the jeers of her peers.

We don't necessarily fit into our world, either. The beauty that God gives us is sometimes very different from the beauty that the world applauds. We lose sight of our God-given beauty when we listen to destructive criticism. As we rest our worth in God's unconditional love, we see ourselves in the light of his truth.

To counterbalance worldly influences, we need to refresh our inner selves with regular positive input. I am a music person—I love to listen to music and sing along with it. Music is a great way to replenish my spirit as I go about my day. Whether with music or something else, find a way to refresh yourself and know Christ's deep love today.

God makes us beautiful.

Surfside Blessings

O our God, we thank you and praise your glorious name!
1 Chronicles 29:13

Ahhhhh! The beauty of the beach! Simple days of high SPF sunscreen and sand between our toes. We never know what to expect from the weather, but it really doesn't matter. The sand wears off the daily grind and the salty air soothes our senses. After a couple of days of salt and sand, the rich beauty of the beach begins to soak in.

Daily life wears us down and dulls our senses. It is hard for us to perceive God's love and protection amidst our spinning days. So often, we are like the sand crabs that scuttle about the sand at twilight. With claws poised to ward off social intrusions, they busily retrieve food and burrow back into their holes, missing the most glorious sunsets!

It's hard to avoid being lonely and crabby in our crazy world. When we disengage from the grind, we are free to connect with God and with others. God is the light that brightens our days, and he longs to bless us with good things. God loves us more than we could ever imagine, so he hopes that we'll enjoy his painting of love in the setting sun.

Reconnect with God and loved ones.

Speak Up!

One night the Lord spoke to Paul in a vision and told him, "Don't be afraid! Speak out! Don't be silent! For I am with you."   Acts 18:9-10

Do you ever wonder about the purpose of being on earth? From our perspective, we are born, live a short while, and die, but there is much more to our existence!

God dreamed each of us up, before time began, to be his companions. Life is much richer when we have someone to share it with, right? God wants to share his existence with us, and he loves each of us as if we were the only one!

God hopes that we'll choose to walk his way each day and hang out with him in this thing called life. Just as love from a child is much richer when the child offers it without being forced, God lets each of us choose whether to love him or not.

When we discover the rich life available in loving God, it is natural to share the news with others who are struggling. Our purpose is to love God and love others. Make your mark by helping others to discover a reason for living.

Speak up about God's love!

Spirit of Praise

If they kept quiet, the stones along the road would burst into cheers! Luke 19:40

The world outdoors has been transformed into a sanctuary of springtime beauty. The flowering trees scatter their perfumed petals on the breeze, the tulips brighten the green grass with lipstick colors, and puffy white clouds dance against the clean blue sky. Despite the beauty outdoors, it is easy to be overwhelmed inside, forget all our blessings, and focus only on ourselves. When we lift our eyes off ourselves, we receive God's power and peace and can offer our gifts of praise.

God has made all of creation to praise him. Jesus said that if no person gave praise to God for who he is, the rocks would burst out and praise him!

Delicate, colorful beauty emerges from deadened brown stalks, and every flower praises God; each blooming flower reminds us of the new life we find in Jesus' death and resurrection.

When we slow down enough to see the beauty of God's creation, we can see how much God loves us. He wants to bring his wholeness, peace, and joy to reign in our lives.

We have reason to praise God!

The Checkout Lane

Your royal husband delights in your beauty; honor him, for he is your lord.   Psalm 45:11

Every time we push the cart into the grocery store checkout lane, we are bombarded by temptation. The candy always hits kids at eye level. How can they not want to buy the brightly colored candy to take home when that is the only thing they see as we pay for our groceries! The giant temptations for women—magazines and tabloids—are conveniently located at our eye level. How could we not compare our bodies and our lives with images of the world's beautiful people? Celebrities look so perfect that our real lives seem inadequate by comparison.

We often put ourselves down as the result of constant comparison, trying to see how we measure up against others. Regardless of how it seems, however, no one is perfect. And regardless of how we compare ourselves with others, only God's opinion really counts.

God is captivated! He made each of us to be exactly as he wanted us to be. He says that we are his "masterpiece" (Ephesians 2:10).

When our lives are full, balanced, and healthy, our true beauty shines through. God is delighted with us!

Believe in the beauty God gave you!

Cinderella Syndrome

My purpose is to give them a rich and satisfying life.
John 10:10

Every little girl loves the Cinderella story—the fairy godmother, the late-night ball, the beautiful gown and the glass slipper, and most of all, the dream of happily ever after. From the time we can wear a tiara and play dress up in frothy gowns and feather boas, every girl longs to be discovered, desired, and rescued from the cinders.

Jesus says that he came to fulfill our lives (see John 10:10). In Cinderella terms, he is the Prince who rescues us from sweeping ashes. Jesus wants us to live happily ever after. We don't have to put a joyful life on hold until we get to heaven. Jesus was not talking about "someday" but about today.

Cinderella could have retreated to her ashes, and we can choose to return to our old lives after we meet our Prince. We know, however, that we are made for more than the meaningless daily repetitions and hopeless frustrations of life. That "something more" is the joy of daily life with Jesus.

Choose to live richly with your Prince, Jesus. He calls you out of the ashes to a brand new life.

We are wired for happily ev........

Welcoming Entry

Welcome [others] with Christian love and with great joy.
Philippians 2:29

About this time every year, I get the itch to replant our
doorstep containers with a few fresh flowers. Of course,
with the departure of frosty weather and the onset of
spring, plant nurseries and grocery stores offer rainbows
of annuals, so it is easy to buy a few to spruce up the yard.
With great soil, a few plants well suited to the shady conditions, and a soaking of water, we easily transform our front
entry into a welcoming place to greet visitors and friends
with a warm hug and a smile.

Warming the entry to our home creates an inviting
entrance to our lives. We naturally feel drawn to a neat and
well-kept front door, and to smiling people rather than
those closed off with a frown. When we plant the beautiful
flowers of a welcoming attitude in our lives, we extend a
warm invitation of love and acceptance to those we greet.
Others will always feel welcome in our lives when we smile
and accept them for who they are. Welcome others into
your life today.

A smile gives a warm welcome.

Momentary Blessings

You will show me the way of life, granting me the joy of your presence and the pleasures of living with you forever.   Psalm 16:11

Often, as we go about our days, our paths seem unfamiliar and we cannot see our way. Where is God in the monotonous routine of our daily lives?

When we focus on ourselves, we miss the truth of our situations. Surely there are parts of our lives that we could be thankful for. Wherever we have missed joy, we have missed the gift that God has given us today.

We may be so obsessed with what did not go as planned that we miss the beauty of the sunrise on our way to work, the trusting smile on a child's face, or the butterfly dancing in the breeze. God uses such details to touch our days and say that he loves us. We may not understand how God fits into our daily routines, but God has a deep, joy-filled life planned for each of us. To see his hand guiding our paths, we have to open our lives to the blessings he places in each moment and realize that he is with us today.

God holds your life in his hands.

Off a Key

No one can lay any foundation other than the one we already have—Jesus Christ.　　　　1 Corinthians 3:11

Typing has come a long way in the past few decades. Now, with keyboarding words into tiny cell phones and data organizers, typing is changing yet again. One thing remains the same: When we place our well-trained fingers on the correct starting keys, the rest of our keystrokes come out as we want them to. Consider that "krdid od pit jp,r lru" is the same fingering as "Jesus is our home key," with the fingers off centered by one key. When we have our fingers in the wrong starting position, the message is garbled.

The same principle applies to our lives. When we are centered on the right key—on Jesus and his love—everything else in life falls into place. Without Jesus, our lives soon become jumbled.

Jesus is our reason for living. Start your day on the right key by connecting with him each morning. A life in relationship to Jesus has meaning, whereas "foundations" of wealth, fame, success, and possessions cannot fulfill us. Set your life on the foundation of Jesus Christ and allow the other things in your life to fall into their proper places.

Jesus is the key to our lives.

Outdoor Time

Then the LORD God planted a garden in Eden in the east, and there he placed the man he had made.

Genesis 2:8

Many of us receive catalogs. Most of mine get pitched, but the cover of one catalog I received was quite beautiful and alluring. It simply read, "Spend More Time Outdoors." The background showed a table under a large, striped umbrella beside a shining blue body of water and a colorful garden. Such simple beauty creates a desire to be outdoors and connect in some way with nature.

God did not place Adam and Eve in a skyscraper or on a crowded street. He did not place them in a noisy office or in front of a television. God placed Adam and Eve in the beautiful and tranquil surroundings of his garden.

We long to spend more time outdoors. As we enjoy nature in all of its beauty, we experience God. Outdoors we experience the peace and serenity of connecting with God through the world he created.

This spring, spend more time outdoors. Walk through a park after work, or eat lunch on a blanket spread in the grass. The possibilities are endless. . . . Take time to connect with God outdoors.

God made the outdoors for our pleasure.

Garden Pleasures

The LORD God placed the man in the Garden of Eden to tend and watch over it.   Genesis 2:15

Some of my most enjoyable time is spent outdoors in the backyard. Every spring, I turn another section of grass into yet another garden. Digging up grass is hard work, so I use the "lasagna" method of garden-starting: Lay down a garden hose in the desired shape and size, cover the entire area with five to ten sheets of newspaper (wet down if it is windy), and spread a two- to three-inch layer of mulch over the newspaper. While the newspaper decomposes, the grass underneath dies. Then you can plant the garden of your dreams! Try sun-loving plants such as daylilies, liatris, echinacea, scabiosa, Becky daisies, Russian sage, and daffodils for a beautiful combination. For a shady site, try hosta, astilbe, dicentra, and heuchera.

Planting a garden and watching it grow into something beautiful is very rewarding. God put Adam and Eve on earth to take pleasure in tending his garden.

Make the world a more beautiful place today! Choose a windowsill herb garden, a balcony plant box, a newspaper-covered garden over suburban grass, or an acre of beauty in the country. Create your pocketful of paradise and enjoy it all season.

Create a garden paradise.

Garden Therapy

I made gardens and parks, filling them with all kinds of fruit trees. Ecclesiastes 2:5

Many people gain pleasure from working in their gardens. Cultivating the soil, tending plants, and pulling weeds frees the soul from life's burdens. After I tend the thorny rosebushes, the thorns of life fade away or lose their grip. Gardening is great therapy for the soul, a great way to turn thoughts to God, gain his perspective, and connect with Jesus in prayer.

We all have someplace that speaks to our souls, a place where God can meet us and soothe our worried minds. For our lives to be healthy, we must renew them frequently in places of beauty where we can connect with our loving God.

Solomon, the renowned king and David's wise son, wrote the book of Ecclesiastes to reveal his own search for meaning and satisfaction in life. After trying just about everything that life offers, his conclusion was that life without God has no meaning (see Ecclesiastes 2:24-26). When we include God in all things and live according to his plan, our lives have significance.

Include God in all that you do, and enrich your life.

God makes our lives meaningful.

May Day

O LORD, what a variety of things you have made!
                                        Psalm 104:24

Every spring, a delightful old-fashioned holiday returns. Handing out May baskets is a beautiful way to celebrate May Day with your friends, family, and neighbors. A simple May basket might consist of a decorated basket or another container filled with flowers, candies, cookies, or other goodies to brighten a friend's day. What a beautiful opportunity to slow down and touch others' lives with the fragrance and joy of springtime!

As you prepare a May basket, a pot of newly planted flowers, or a jar for your table filled with cut flowers from the garden, remember Jesus as you celebrate the rebirth of spring. Martin Luther once said, "Our Lord has written the promise of the resurrection not in words alone, but in every leaf in springtime." Spread Jesus' love as you witness the beauty and fragrance of this spring.

If we lived to be one hundred, we would only experience the miracle of nature's rebirth one hundred times! Enjoy the fresh fragrance of daffodils, the peonies laden with dew and perfume, and the tulips gracefully bending toward the spring sun. Store up the freshness and beauty for less sunny days, and share springtime with your loved ones today.

Share the blessings of spring.

Misfit Mallards

Do not love this world nor the things it offers you.

1 John 2:15

Every spring, an unusual phenomenon occurs in our neighbors' backyard: A pair of ducks takes over their swimming pool as their own private pond. It is funny from our side of the fence, but probably not for our neighbors! The ducks quack, quack, quack their way in for a landing in the little pool dozens of times a day.

At times, Mr. and Mrs. Mallard can be caught eating from beneath our backyard bird feeder. It is funny to see mallard ducks waddling about among the cardinals, sparrows, flickers, and finches.

In the same way that we smile at the sight of misfit mallards, God must smile as he looks upon our daily lives. He watches us as we go about our days trying to fit into a world predominantly focused on living without God. As hard as we try, we won't ever feel completely at home with what this world has to offer. God has so much more waiting for us in heaven—the best is yet to come!

We will be at home in heaven.

Time to Talk

I will answer them before they even call to me. While they are still talking about their needs, I will go ahead and answer their prayers! Isaiah 65:24

Communication is vital to every relationship. To know our spouses, we spend time with them in conversation. To learn about our children, we listen to their dreams and desires. We grow closer to a friend by chatting over coffee. We deepen our relationship with God by connecting with him in prayer.

Prayer is one of the resources God has given us for staying connected with him—it is our indispensable spiritual lifeline. In prayer, we turn our thoughts to God and communicate with him honestly, as with a friend.

We can pray anywhere, at any time. We can call on God to comfort our troubled hearts. When we need reassurance, we can listen for the gentle whisper of love that he offers. When we are filled with gratitude to God, we can lift up our hearts in praise and thanks for who he is and what he's done for us. God knows us and wants us to know him. He loves to answer prayers, so give him your burdens today.

Offer Jesus your prayerful heart.

Sunny Daisies

The righteous will shine like the sun in their Father's Kingdom.   Matthew 13:43

I love a daisy's sunny disposition. Regardless of the weather, its face is always smiling. Even in the rain, daisies stand up tall, still beaming; they praise the Creator with their beauty and thank him for their time to bloom. This is inspiring. It seems impossible for us to shine regardless of the weather in our own lives, but even when things don't go our way, we can choose joy. We can choose our attitude toward what comes along.

Jesus is our example, and we learn from his life. He had many things going on, but he was never hurried. He endured difficult encounters, demanding people, and draining situations every day, but he was never stressed out or frazzled. Although he had the responsibility for mankind's salvation on his shoulders, he never collapsed or broke into a million pieces. He simply trusted God.

What a wonderful way to live . . . with less stress, less hurry, and fewer frazzles! May we choose life's course as Jesus did, by trusting God to put the pieces in their proper place.

Jesus never rushed or hurried.

Whirlybirds

They are like trees planted along the riverbank, bearing fruit each season.   Psalm 1:3

Set free by gentle breezes, the seeds of maple trees set sail at this time of year. Round and round they whirl, resting at last on the ground. Like little helicopters twirling softly through the air, whirlybirds are one of the beautiful miracles found during the spring. We marvel at God's intricate creation in each sturdy flying maple seed. God even knows the number of seeds that a single tree will yield!

Like whirlybirds, we are each formed to spread our wings and fly. God created each of us to make our unique mark on the world. Only God can enable us to reach our full potential, and only he knows the number of lives that will be influenced for him as a result of our lives.

The author of Psalm 1 likens a person who follows God's lead to a fruitful tree.

When we delight in God and in his Word, we are able to soar to our full potential and bear much fruit in our lives. Take joy in your creation and take courage—spread your wings and fly!

Spread your wings and fly!

Fragrant Offering

You neglected the courtesy of olive oil to anoint my head, but she has anointed my feet with rare perfume.

Luke 7:46

What a beautiful time of year for strolling through a park or garden! The lilacs are filling the breeze with their delicious fragrance. From a distance, lilacs don't attract much attention, but what appears from afar as one large blue or purple flower is actually a gathering of hundreds of tiny starlike blossoms that shine in the sun.

Just as lilac blossoms fill a room with their fragrance and beauty, our lives radiate beauty when we're shining inside and out.

In Luke 7, a woman approached Jesus with overflowing love and gratitude. In humility and gentleness, she poured a fragrant perfume over Jesus' feet. Leaving behind practicality and doubt, the woman offered her best as a gift to Jesus.

We can respond to Jesus' love each day by pouring out the best of our lives as a fragrant offering to him. We allow God's love to radiate from our lives when our hearts are full of gratitude to him.

Jesus appreciates our love and devotion.

Honoring Mom

Your people will be my people, and your God will be my God.
                                                    Ruth 1:16

In a country far from her own, Naomi grieved the loss of her husband and two sons. She was surprised when her widowed daughter-in-law Ruth offered to accompany her as she journeyed back to Israel, her home country. Ruth loved her mother-in-law and was drawn to the God that Naomi worshipped.

Once they were in Israel, the women needed food. Through God's leading and Naomi's encouragement, Ruth gathered leftover wheat from the fields owned by a man named Boaz. Over the following months, and with Naomi's continuing encouragement, Ruth and Boaz came to love each other and wed. By letting go of her only kin and releasing Ruth to remarry, Naomi influenced a great ancestry, for through the marriage of Ruth and Boaz came their great-grandson David and eventually Jesus the Messiah!

Mothers have a profound impact on the lives of their children through their ongoing encouragement, love, and acceptance. The love, respect, and devotion between mothers and their children are some of God's greatest blessings. When mothers release their children to become all they are intended to be, great hearts for God often result.

Loving moms encourage us.

Listening by the Creek

All who listen to me will live in peace, untroubled by fear of harm.   Proverbs 1:33

When I was a girl, I loved to go to a soothing spot by the creek and listen. Now, as an adult, I love hiking or walking to replenish my soul, or sitting in my favorite chair with my journal. The habit of journaling brings inner thoughts into the light of day, and this helps tremendously in sorting life out. In the midst of life's mystery, it is encouraging to look back and remember how faithful God has been through each joy and trial.

Allow yourself some time today just to *be* in God's presence. Let your soul catch up with your body and be filled with God's peace. Instead of bouncing from one activity to the next, let your roots grow a bit deeper by taking time to reflect and to express your feelings and thoughts to God in prayer.

Make room in your life for a breather. Even ten minutes of quiet can slow you down and bring you closer to the life you long for. When your life is intimately connected with God, his peace and joy will bless your day!

Slow down and listen to God.

Becoming Mom

The master was full of praise. "Well done, my good and faithful servant. You have been faithful in handling this small amount, so now I will give you many more responsibilities."
Matthew 25:21

In honor of mothers everywhere on Mother's Day, we remember the sacrifices they made and the dreams they passed on to our own lives.

Expectant moms anticipate the big arrival by decorating the baby's room, selecting tiny clothes, choosing names, and packing the hospital bag. As the preparations are made, the learning begins.

Moms pop pacifiers back in place for the tenth time every night and learn patience. From the trusting hands of little ones, moms learn faith. A glimpse of sleeping babies teaches moms peace. In the rolling-belly laugh of toddler tickles, moms discover pure joy.

Surely God designed a mom's role to make them more mature and more like Jesus. Moms certainly know the meaning of being a servant! As moms become more like Jesus, they can look forward to hearing God's "well done." In all of life, character develops as we are tested, tried, and stretched. Thank your mom for her gifts of love and sacrifice!

Motherhood is a gift from God!

Media Messages

Everything is pure to those whose hearts are pure. But nothing is pure to those who are corrupt and unbelieving, because their minds and consciences are corrupted.   Titus 1:15

Just as parents screen what their children see and hear, we also need to monitor what we watch and listen to. Positive, encouraging input leads to positive, encouraging output in actions and attitudes, and "garbage in, garbage out" also holds true. The attitudes and beliefs of the company we keep affect our inner lives.

We women can watch soap operas, chick flicks, talk shows, celebrity reviews, and fashion shows. Though some of these add value to our lives, we need to monitor the attitudes that result from these influences. We may have unrealistic expectations of real relationships based on romantically scripted chick flicks, for example. It is easier to spend hours watching imaginary relationships on the screen than to attend to the real relationships that God has placed in our lives.

Entertainment is important, but intellectual smog negatively affects our mental and spiritual health. The love and joy gained from real-life devotion are based on God and his love for us.

Invest your attention in your loved ones today.

River of Words

Whatever is in your heart determines what you say.

Matthew 12:34

When I was a kid, our yard backed up to a spring-fed stream. All summer, the water was clear, clean, cold, and refreshing. One year, the stream became foul smelling and cloudy. A chemical truck had wrongfully disposed of its contents in our stream. Our once pure springwater was now repulsive. To clean up the mess, the pollution had to be cleansed at the source.

Jesus said, "A good person produces good things from the treasury of a good heart, and an evil person produces evil things from the treasury of an evil heart" (Matthew 12:35). What comes down the stream reveals what is at its source, and what comes out of our mouths reveals what is in our hearts. We often hear destructive speech coming from ourselves or others. Such speech boldly declares that our hearts are a mess.

As cleaning up a polluted stream begins at its source, cleaning up our language must start with our attitudes. Today, pray that God will change your attitudes for the better. As God fills your heart with his love and presence, your speech will refresh and encourage others.

Jesus can cleanse your heart.

Caterpillar to Butterfly

Don't copy the behavior and customs of this world, but let God transform you into a new person by changing the way you think. Romans 12:2

Decked out in black, white, and school-bus yellow stripes, the last monarch caterpillar chomped its way through the swamp milkweed plant in our backyard. We brought it in to save it from the birds and watched wide-eyed as our striped houseguest wriggled from its caterpillar skin into a chrysalis. Days passed as the chrysalis hung silent and still.

About two weeks later, Madeleine Monarch emerged. Over the next few hours, her transformation continued as she stretched and dried. When she was ready to fly, we set her on the climbing rose in our yard. She flapped and flapped, and we rejoiced with her when she finally took flight!

From crawling creature to fluttering magnificence, God's butterfly transformation is awe-inspiring. God also wants to give us wings. The butterfly's transformation occurs in silence and waiting, and human change also happens in stillness. God uses our current circumstances to prepare us for what will come next. Allow him to prepare you and give you wings to soar up to your dreams.

God prepares us for things to come.

Smooth Sailing

*When you go through deep waters, I will be with you.
When you go through rivers of difficulty, you will not
drown.*   Isaiah 43:2

Our family loves to go sailing on beautiful weekend days.
When the sky is blue and there is a bit of a breeze, we can
relax and enjoy smooth sailing under the late spring sun.

We often hope and pray that our lives will sail smoothly,
and that disappointment and obstacles, discouragement
and delays won't hinder our plans. But days of smooth
sailing don't last forever; God uses the storms of our lives
to help us grow, to make us better sailors, to give us confidence, and to reveal himself to us.

Remember the disciples' stormy sail across the Sea of
Galilee? They panicked when the sailing became rough,
and they doubted Jesus' care. Jesus calmed their storm, just
as he helps us to deal with the chaos in our hearts and lives.

During the storms of our lives, it is easy to panic, but
God is on board. He hasn't jumped ship, forgotten us, or
left us behind. God promises to be with us! We can be sure
that he is there.

God is with us on stormy days.

Good Soil

Still other seed fell on fertile soil. This seed grew and produced a crop that was a hundred times as much as had been planted!   Luke 8:8

Planting instructions come with the new roses that arrive on my doorstep each year. It is said that a rose is only as good as the soil it is planted in. When a gardener prepares a new rose site with rich soil, good drainage, and full sun, the rose will thrive. Well-tended roses will bear more flowers and be more disease resistant, winter hardy, and fragrant. Since I learned this lesson the hard way, I heed the planting directions, and by taking more time and care in preparation, I enjoy more magnificent blooms.

As roses planted in good soil produce a better crop, God's Word planted in the fertile soil of humble hearts produces a more fruitful faith. Jesus said, "The seeds that fell on the good soil represent honest, good-hearted people who hear God's word, cling to it, and patiently produce a huge harvest" (Luke 8:15).

When we follow Jesus and listen to his Word, he produces beautiful fruit in our lives. Take time today to prepare a good site in your heart, and you will enjoy a huge harvest of faith.

We are nurtured by God's Word.

Complete Acceptance

Your love for one another will prove to the world that you are my disciples. John 13:35

As humans, we often feel uncomfortable with people who are different from us. When we feel uncomfortable, we may also feel insecure in ourselves. We wonder, *Do I still measure up? Are they better than me?* To ensure that we are better, we sometimes put other people down.

Jesus said that others will recognize us as his followers because of our love. Such love is unconditional, which means that we love others as Jesus does, no matter what. If we are to be filled with Jesus' love, we must accept others for who they are, completely and unconditionally. We accept those who are different by serving and encouraging them, reaching out and loving them in the way that Christ loves us. Christ doesn't see any one of us as better than another. Jesus knows that we are all imperfect and in need of a Savior.

When we know God's acceptance of us, we can accept others. We will want to share God's amazing love with them as we embrace their differences and love them for who they are—people who are treasured by God!

Accept others despite their differences.

Butterfly Beauty

You should clothe yourselves instead with the beauty that comes from within, the unfading beauty of a gentle and quiet spirit, which is so precious to God.   1 Peter 3:4

As I allow my mind to rest on an image of wholeness, I picture a beautiful butterfly, a tiger swallowtail that visited my yard recently.

I watched this delicate beauty make her way about the privet. The swallowtail was damaged—nearly half of her wing was missing—but she didn't seem to complain. In her unhurried and graceful manner, she allowed the sunlight to shine through her delicately painted wings as she brought a quiet beauty into my world. In the tiger swallowtail, beauty is found in wholeness, not in perfection. She let the light shine through her uniquely broken beauty.

We imperfect humans would do well to learn from the butterfly's simple, quiet beauty. We are not perfect, but we can allow the Son's light to shine through our lives so that a rare, beautiful wholeness fills our world. Beauty is found in kindness and growth from within, not in criticizing other people. True beauty shines through our imperfections; it withstands all seasons of life.

True beauty is found within.

Monarch or Viceroy?

The Son of Man, on the other hand, feasts and drinks, and you say, "He's a glutton and a drunkard, and a friend of tax collectors and other sinners!" Luke 7:34

I love to photograph my garden—especially the butterflies and hummingbirds. They are very difficult to photograph, but when I can capture a close-up, it takes my breath away. I recently photographed what I thought was a monarch. A little investigation convinced me that the butterfly was really a viceroy.

Intrigued, I dug deeper into my butterfly book and learned that viceroys are clever little creatures. To fool hungry birds, viceroys dress to resemble monarch butterflies. Their only distinguishing mark is an extra curve on their hind wings. Birds don't like monarchs, which are foul tasting from eating the asclepias plant as caterpillars, so the viceroy protects itself in this way.

As humans, the only distinguishing mark of our lives' allegiance is on our hearts. Jesus was judged unworthy by the religious holier-than-thous of his day, but God sees what lies within. Today, accept others regardless of their outer markings. We are all longing to fly free and be accepted.

Jesus loves us each for who we are.

Free Home Furnishings

Everyone who asks, receives. Everyone who seeks, finds. And to everyone who knocks, the door will be opened.   Matthew 7:8

Imagine parking your car at the nearby grocery store. When you walk inside to grab a cart, you are greeted by the store manager. Because you have come, you have won a fully paid houseful of designer furniture, and all you have to do is say yes. *Wow,* you think, *a new designer interior for my home. I didn't have to pay. . . . I don't deserve it . . . but, okay! Yes!* And it is done. Your home is changed forever, and you can fully enjoy it.

   Here's a story that's actually true: God is smitten with you and me. He longs to show us his love and generosity just for showing up at his door and accepting his offer of a grander life. When we say yes to God's offer, he takes out the old furnishings and fills our lives with love, peace, and joy. We didn't pay for it and we don't deserve it, but our lives are changed forever. Because of his gift, we will enjoy life forever in the greatness and beauty of heaven with Jesus.

Jesus freely offers us life.

The Criminal on the Cross

Then he said, "Jesus, remember me when you come into your Kingdom." And Jesus replied, "I assure you, today you will be with me in paradise."　　　Luke 23:42-43

Getting into heaven is not based on what church we go to, how regularly we go, who our friends are, how much we give away, where we live, what kind of car we drive, how much missionary time we serve, what kinds of food we eat, or what we do or don't drink. It is based on our hearts.

The criminal on the cross beside Jesus probably did nothing that we perceive as being right, but Jesus accepted him in the last hour. The criminal turned humbly to Jesus and asked for forgiveness, and Jesus said, "I assure you, today you will be with me in paradise."

It did not matter to Jesus that the criminal had made a mess of his life. His crimes did not disqualify him from Jesus' love and acceptance.

No matter where you have come from, what you have done, or what state your life is in, Jesus will accept you and offer you paradise with him forever. Accept Jesus' offer and build a new life with him.

Jesus accepts all of us.

The Sparrow

*What is the price of two sparrows—one copper coin?
But not a single sparrow can fall to the ground without
your Father knowing it. And the very hairs on your head
are all numbered. So don't be afraid; you are more
valuable to God than a whole flock of sparrows.*

Matthew 10:29-31

The birdbath fountain looks beautiful from our breakfast
table and provides a tranquil scene to watch when we're
sitting there. Softly and silently, birds come and go, stoop-
ing, sipping, and resting. One spring day, the scene was
rather more raucous than peaceful. Our boxer, Jesse, was
having some fun with a bird. When I rescued it, the tiny
sparrow was tired but unharmed.

So often in today's world, we are caught up in terrifying events and heart-wrenching problems. In the midst of
uncertainty, we can rest in knowing that God watches over
the sparrows. How much more will he guard us and care
for every detail of our lives! According to Jesus, nothing
could happen to a sparrow without God knowing it. God
cares so much for us that he knows the number of hairs
on our heads. Lay down your worries and trust in the God
who cares for you.

God cares for us.

Looney Toons Taz

Times of refreshment will come from the presence of the Lord.
Acts 3:20

Looney Toons cartoons, with Bugs Bunny and Daffy Duck, always get a laugh with their banter. Taz, the Tasmanian devil, is a hit at our house. He bounces off walls, spins like a tornado, and blazes through anything in his path.

Taz reminds me of how we live today. Can't you just see it? The alarm is the "Go!" pistol that starts our race toward the day's finish line. And we're off! We shower, dress, care for loved ones, and race out the door, twist-turning Taz-style to our next destination, cell phone in one hand and breakfast in the other. All day, we bounce off walls and blaze through everything in our paths, giving folks a cordial wave as we blaze off to the next activity.

Are you getting ragged, with no time to replenish and no energy left to enjoy your life, much less grow? Think of something you really want to do—lunch with a friend, a sail on a nearby lake, a picnic with your family in the park—that will refresh your spirit. Clear a space in your schedule and connect with someone you love today.

Slow down and refuel your spirit.

Wilting in the Heat

When the king smiles, there is life; his favor refreshes like a spring rain.   Proverbs 16:15

An early heat wave has come upon our area and our garden hoses aren't even out yet. In area gardens, newly planted annuals are already wilting, their roots dry and blossoms drooping. Instead of growing and blooming, plants under stress curl inward to conserve energy.

Every day, we are stretched by the demands of our lives—kids, husbands, coworkers, PTA parents, teachers, doctors, bankers, you name it. When we encounter these stressors, we also turn inward to survive. No one can give 100 percent without having to slow down and refuel.

It is wise to take time out before we burn out. When we are speeding along doing so many things, we cannot expect to enjoy our lives or use the gifts that God has given us.

We were born to grow, bloom, and touch the world with our uniqueness. Ask God to help you slow down and replenish your spirit. Get in the habit of doing something that refreshes you—take a walk, paint a canvas, read a book. God's life-giving love will enable you to grow, bloom, and enjoy this day!

A sustainable life energizes us.

Dime-Store Beads

Pursue righteous living, faithfulness, love, and peace.
Enjoy the companionship of those who call on the Lord
with pure hearts. 2 Timothy 2:22

It is easy to fritter our lives away. We get caught up in
the cheap, shiny plastic beads of life found in the nickel
gumball machine rather than appreciate the precious pearls
of our real lives. We often pursue elusive-but-glorious titles
and awards rather than enjoy the smaller moments that
make life rich.

Humans like to feel important. Sometimes, by investing
our time in things that make us feel desired and needed, we
move away from the source of true meaning, and further
still from the earthly relationships we need and long for.
When we make glory our goal, and not the experiences and
relationships formed in the process, we pass up pearls for
dime-store beads.

Examine your goals today. Life frittered away by a
hectic schedule or a powerful position will never bring the
life you long for. Choose to invest your life in rich relationships and to enjoy the journey. Having loved ones to share
the ride of life will bring the true pearls of beautiful meaning into your life.

Share life with your loved ones.

Simplify the Schedule

Then Jesus said, "Let's go off by ourselves to a quiet place and rest awhile." He said this because there were so many people coming and going that Jesus and his apostles didn't even have time to eat. Mark 6:31

What is the answer to all this rushing about? Jesus was very much in demand in his day. Crowds constantly followed him for his healing and teaching. Jesus knew that, in order for his ministry to be better than mediocre, he had to stop in the middle of the rush to refuel his spirit.

How can we simplify our schedules? Here's a plan: List all the items on your calendar and find a few events that you can eliminate. Reflect on that change and simplify some more until your life feels fulfilled rather than hurried and your spirit feels abundant rather than depleted.

Getting rid of clutter will help you focus on the essential aspects of your life. Let God direct you into situations where your heart sings and you can be at your best. In doing so, you will receive God's abundant blessing, and your days will be much richer for the effort!

Jesus encourages time for rest.

In Remembrance

Ten lepers stood at a distance, crying out, "Jesus, Master, have mercy on us!" He looked at them and said, "Go show yourselves to the priests." And as they went, they were cleansed of their leprosy. Luke 17:12-14

How often do we lose something ordinary yet necessary for everyday life, such as our keys? Inevitably, after searching for what seems like an eternity and being well past late for something, we discover what we lost. Things are usually misplaced because we forget to put things in their proper place.

As we grow older, we excuse our forgetfulness by speaking of "senior moments," but in truth, it is human nature to forget, regardless of our age.

Jesus had compassion on ten lepers and healed their leprosy. Their lives were forever changed for the better, and by the time they reached the priest who certified their rehabilitation, they were restored to health. "One of them, when he saw that he was healed, came back to Jesus, shouting, 'Praise God!'" (Luke 17:15). The other nine forgot to thank Jesus for restoring their lives.

In the excitement and busyness of life, we often forget the blessings we've been given. We have so much to be thankful for! As Memorial Day approaches, remember and give thanks.

Thank those who sacrifice for you.

Pass-Along Plants

Their trust should be in God, who richly gives us all we need for our enjoyment. . . . [Be] generous to those in need, always being ready to share with others.

1 Timothy 6:17-18

Gardening is a great hobby to share with others. Every spring, avid gardeners divide and move many plants. In every new garden, bare soil and small plants are prominent, but perennial plants mature and have to be split to remain healthy. When gardeners divide many plants, they naturally want to share. There are always extras to pass along to gardening friends.

I love to receive new plants to nestle into my garden. Even more, I enjoy passing extras along to friends and seeing their faces light up. Once we've received pass-along plants, we have a sweet reminder of our friends blooming in our garden. In my own gardens, I cherish the daisies from Julie's garden and irises from the neighbor's.

God's generosity is much like that of gardening friends. Blessings always overflow from his pass-along joy. We only have to let him know that we are interested in receiving his blessings to have more than we could ever need, with plenty of love to share with friends as well.

God provides everything we need.

Boosts of Love

If someone says, "I love God," but hates a Christian brother or sister, that person is a liar; for if we don't love people we can see, how can we love God, whom we cannot see?

1 John 4:20

Every gardening book recommends plant food for bigger blooms and healthier plants. Many people claim to have miraculous results from banana peels and coffee grounds, but I usually stick with the tried-and-true, easy-to-throw-on granular fertilizer. With one or two helpings of fertilizer per season, my gardens bloom very well.

Our relationships also need regular boosts of nourishment—not bagged granular fertilizer, but love and devotion. It is easy to follow our world's prescription for feeding ourselves lots of love, when those we love need our positive words and actions.

Sometimes we go through tough spells in our relationships when it is hard to smile and we have to bite our tongues. To have a healthy relationship, the feedings of love and positive encouragement need to outweigh the tough, negative withdrawals of gritty words and selfish attitudes.

Today, help the garden of your relationships to grow and become healthy. Invest in positive words and attitudes, and you'll be blessed with strong, growing relationships.

Love even in the hard times.

Remember Me

He took some bread and gave thanks to God for it. Then he broke it in pieces . . . saying, "This is my body, which is given for you. Do this to remember me."   Luke 22:19

There are many important things in life for us to remember: birthdays, anniversaries, passwords, addresses and phone numbers, Web sites, appointments, car keys, and names. There is a good reason to remember each of these: to honor someone, to avoid repeating a mistake, to have access, to get where we need to go, to learn something, or to draw close to someone.

Jesus established a beautiful way for us to remember him. Communion helps us to remember Jesus as he emptied himself and gave his life for us. In joining together with others when taking the bread and the cup, we reaffirm our faith and join as a community to remember our Lord.

This Memorial Day, remember your loved ones, those who have given their lives for our freedom, and those who still serve in protecting our country. They have made great sacrifices to maintain our rich lives. Remember Jesus' sacrifice by sharing in Communion.

We remember Jesus in Communion.

Sowing Wildflowers

Jesus . . . wanted to spend more time with his disciples and teach them.   Mark 9:30-31

My favorite children's book, *Miss Rumphius,* tells the story of a woman who spent her days sowing wildflower lupine seeds to leave the world more beautiful than she had found it. This beautiful story inspires readers to share more of themselves.

Most of us focus our entire lives and energy on our income. Of course, at the end of our lives it won't matter how much wealth we have accumulated.

One thing that does matter is whether our lives have been significant. Just one wildflower changes the entire landscape for the better within a few years, and one life of giving to others changes the human landscape forever.

Decide today to make an impact with your life. Don't just accept the status quo, but use what you have to make a difference.

God has given you a gift. Believe it, discover it, develop it, and cherish it. Give it away and spread it around to others. Investing in others is an incredible way to live, and you will receive incredible returns!

Don't live to see what you can get from life. Give of yourself and make a difference!

Jesus invested in his disciples.

Perfect Plans

This is the message of Good News . . . that there is peace with God through Jesus Christ.   Acts 10:36

Life is full of surprises—a perfect vacation interrupted by a Category 4 hurricane, a perfect picnic spoiled by swarms of ants and bees, the perfect visit to friends cut short by illness, the perfectly planned retirement aborted for medical reasons.

When we are taken by surprise amid our perfect plans, we make one of two choices: to roll with the punches and trust that God is truly in control, or take things into our own hands and take out our frustrations on those around us. Surely, trusting God beats the drawbacks of anger, stress, and frustration. This is easier said than done, however, so how do we do it?

We take a look at Jesus' life.

Jesus desired the best for everyone he encountered, yet he did not expect them to be or do as he wished. In his demanding life, Jesus left his concerns, needs, and timing up to God. Jesus did not worry uselessly about people and situations beyond his control. He followed God's lead, stayed close to God, offered his best, and left the rest to God.

Leave the details to God.

Moose in the Road

Lead me in the right path, O LORD. . . . Make your way plain for me to follow.   Psalm 5:8

One summer we camped on Maine's Mount Desert Island, home to beautiful Acadia National Park. Early in the day, we visited many spectacular sights and chatted with a ranger at one of our stops. He said that the likelihood of our seeing a moose on the island was very slim, but when we returned to our campsite that evening, a very large moose was blocking the road. Next to our four-door car, the moose was huge! We were in awe as the moose stood and began its slow, jiggly jog down the road to our camp and eventually into the woods. We had seen Maine's largest living roadblock!

In our lives, the way ahead is often unclear. At other times, our life's path seems obvious, but many obstacles block the way. God's long-range perspective renders the best navigation, so we should follow his path and ask him to keep us from interfering with his plan for our lives. As we trust God, he will clear the way even when roadblocks are large and intimidating. Every obstacle presents a new opportunity—if we are patient and follow God's way.

God helps us overcome obstacles.

Peaceful Pelicans

You will keep in perfect peace all who trust in you, all whose thoughts are fixed on you!   Isaiah 26:3

Have you ever sat on the beach with your toes in the sand, watching the grand pelicans? They are massive birds, but very graceful and serene. On a deserted beach at sunrise or sunset, their powerful wings can be heard beating the air overhead. As they cruise in silent ranks just inches above the surf, they fill me with peace.

Humans hold tight to foolish struggles that don't concern the pelicans. If we were to stop resisting the plans God has for us, could we go with the flow as they do? Might we have fewer conflicts if we could relax in the process of becoming the distinctive individuals God intends us to be? By yielding to God's purpose in our lives, we might learn more about the unexpected things he has in store for us—things that undoubtedly would satisfy our souls. Wouldn't it be wonderful to maintain peace and centeredness, knowing we were following God's plan, despite the tyranny of our daily schedules?

Fix your mind on Jesus. Allow him to bring his work in you to completion, and experience the integrity and authority of becoming your authentic self.

Focus on Jesus.

Climbing Rose

It is I who makes the green tree wither and gives the dead tree new life.   Ezekiel 17:24

I am a rose lover, and early June is a favorite time in our gardens. When I planted a New Dawn rosebush about three years ago, it looked very small next to the huge arbor Brian had built for it. In about two years, the rosebush had climbed to the top, and soon the arbor was covered with heavenly soft-pink blooms. This year the arbor is inundated with velvety pink roses from that same little rosebush. The fragrance gently rises with the breeze.

The Lord of the universe loves to prosper us. From small beginnings, he develops us into strong and blessed people. He is able to grow abundant lives from the small seeds he has planted in our hearts. If we turn the growing process over to him, we "will be enriched in every way so that [we] can always be generous" (2 Corinthians 9:11). God enriches our relationships, health, and finances so that we can share his blessings with others. Allow God to root you in the fertile soil of his love. You will grow tall and beautiful.

God prospers our lives.

Colorful Combinations

Let us not neglect our meeting together, as some people do, but encourage one another. Hebrews 10:25

Each summer morning as I rise, my eyes are drawn to the colors beyond the window. June always brings out the hues I favor in our gardens: blues, magentas, creams, and purples in lovely variations. The tall, green maiden grass, soft spikes of magenta lithrum, silvery-blue and lavender Russian sage, sunny stands of Becky daisies, and cream-colored daylilies enliven the back border. Individually, these plants don't attract much attention, but combined they are spectacular.

We, too, are less effective as individuals than we are when our distinctive gifts join with those of others within a community. Sometimes integrating lives in community is difficult—some personalities, like some colors, clash when put together. When we don't insist on our own way, but encourage one another to become our collective best, we embody Jesus' ideal for the church.

Jesus surrounded himself with friends and followers. He didn't see eye to eye with everyone, but he encouraged others and created a loyal band of followers. Ask him to make you a strong individual who works well with a team.

Be strong in community.

Trust the Hand

The LORD will hold you in his hand for all to see—
a splendid crown in the hand of God.   Isaiah 62:3

The neighbor kids recently rang the doorbell, holding three precious baby robins in their hands and asking for help in caring for them. Apparently, the babies had hopped from their nest near the neighbors' front door when their parents were gone.

All evening, we waited for the robin parents to return to their young, but it became clear that if the babies were to survive, we would have to intervene. While hand-feeding squirmy worms to one robin, our five-year-old asked, "Why do these babies let us feed them when the other birds fly right away?" Great question—these robins seemed to know the hands that fed them.

It is hard to trust the hand that feeds us—the hand of God—but when we live in relationship with him, he lifts us up in his hands and gently cares for us.

Everything that we are and all that we have comes from God's hands. May we rest in their comfort, protection, and provision today, extending God's security and blessing to those around us.

God holds you in his hands.

Unhurried Beauty

Let all that I am wait quietly before God, for my hope is in him. . . . Trust in him at all times.   Psalm 62:5, 8

How many times have I hurried past the quiet beauty of a daisy or a fragrant rose? Too often, my days are dictated by my to-do list, which drives the pace of my life and the state of my attitudes. The pure white beauty of a single daisy draws me to a more centered and grounded space within myself.

Flowers are completely dependent on God for their well-being and growth, but unlike humans, a seed doesn't worry about whether or not the conditions are right for it to germinate. It simply waits for God's appointed time and place. The seedling concentrates completely upon growing strong, without anxiety about being crowded out, trampled upon, or looking less attractive than the next flower. The fledgling plant grows toward the light, allows buds to form, and finally, unfurls its glory.

By simplifying our schedules, we can focus more single-mindedly on our growth in God, and do so without haste or anxiety. Commit your life to God today, and wait for your appointed time to shine.

Wait peacefully on God.

Fulfilled Beauty

*His righteousness will be like a garden in early spring,
with plants springing up everywhere.*   Isaiah 61:11

In many June gardens, roses are blooming profusely. Regal
purples, brilliant pinks, subtle yellows, and pure whites fill
morning breezes with heady fragrance. Each beautiful blossom trusts that its glory will be unveiled and its purpose
will be revealed before its short life comes to an end. God
sustains the natural world and discloses his beauty in
creation to all who pause to observe it.

    God cares for every living creature. He breathes magnif-
icent life into each being. He formed you in your mother's
womb and knew you before time began. Abandon yourself to God—trust, rest, let go, and let our loving Maker
bestow his dazzling life on you.

    Trust means waiting with confidence, knowing that
someone greater is in control of your existence. Trust
invites you to yield your own ideas to the plan of one who
has the whole universe in view.

    Wait upon God to breathe his life into you today. Let
go of striving and filling your schedule to the brim. Release
control of the day's outcome. Trust God to bring your life
to completion.

Wait in confidence.

Gordo the Hummingbird

Give all your worries and cares to God, for he cares about you.   1 Peter 5:7

I could not believe my eyes the first time I witnessed the high-speed chase. They were zipping in and out, up and down, round and round, and nearly colliding at every turn! The tiniest animals in our backyard knocked our socks off with their acrobatic competition. Who were these feisty little creatures? Hummingbirds! The hummer I've named Gordo is so defensive of his feeder that he can't just enjoy what he's been given; he's constantly chasing off every other hummingbird that comes to feed!

My pretty little hummer illustrates a very human dilemma. Often we are so preoccupied with protecting our property and defending our rights that we cannot enjoy our very abundant lives. God provides for us, just as I provide food for my hummingbirds. In the same way I make sure that Gordo has enough food, God is even more mindful of caring for our needs. Instead of hoarding our gifts, we can share them with others. Instead of frantically performing to ensure that we have enough, we can trust God to look after our lives.

When we let go and trust, stress and anxiety evaporate from our lives.

God provides everything we need.

All in the Release

Give your burdens to the L<small>ORD</small>, and he will take care of you.
Psalm 55:22

Fishing season makes for great family memories at the neighborhood pond. One year, to be helpful, I took up pole duties. Yes, I even threaded the squirming worms, and then I took up the pole to help cast. I'm not sure if I had forgotten how to cast effectively or if our two-foot Scooby-Doo pole was a dud, but casting wasn't as easy as it looks on those fishing shows. My cast eventually reached the water, but only because I tried again and again to release properly.

We hold tightly to our many problems—about work, children, money—fretting about them deep into the night. We also cling to our life dreams about our homes, families, relationships, work, and financial security.

Psalm 55 tells us to release our cares to God. Just as casting places the hook in the pond, releasing our cares to God places them in his hands. Unless we learn to release, we will never know the joy of the catch: the deep knowledge that we are doing and being what we were made for. What can you release to God today?

Release your worries to God.

Crab-Apple Tree of Comparison

Pay careful attention to your own work, for then you will get the satisfaction of a job well done, and you won't need to compare yourself to anyone else. Galatians 6:4

Tall trees, short trees, flowering trees, fruiting trees—trees come in every shape and size, just like people. Do trees compare themselves to one another as humans do? Does the blazing red maple feel superior to the shaggy river birch? Does the crab apple become crabby about its small, round shape as compared to the stately oak?

Humans compare themselves with others. We want to know how we measure up. An A student would not feel as superior if there were no B, C, D, or F. Comparisons also leave someone feeling inferior. God does not buy into either—he created each of us equal.

Since we all have the need to feel valuable, we should let God validate our worth. God's opinion is the one that really matters. We know that he loves us completely—win or lose, succeed or fail. Success in God's eyes is becoming all that he made us to be.

Today, rise above crabby comparisons and derive your true worth from God.

Comparison hinders a full life.

Learning Love

Love is patient and kind. Love is not jealous or boastful or proud or rude. It does not demand its own way. It is not irritable, and it keeps no record of being wronged.

1 Corinthians 13:4-5

Stories told from one generation to another are blessings. It is such fun to hear what it was like when those who lived before us were young. Brian recently read aloud from a book his grandmother wrote about her childhood. Stories of goats ramming her aunt, chickens in the house, and a shoe used to get them back in line made us laugh out loud as we envisioned life in her day.

Remembering those who go before us is an act of love. Love is the essential oil that soothes our family relationships. With love, we don't have to have our own way; we can think first of someone else's needs. We can celebrate someone else's successes without becoming jealous and resentful. We can practice smiling in the morning in place of the grouchy irritability that comes so naturally. We can forgive mistakes and move on, knowing that we are not perfect, either.

Today, remember your ancestors with gratitude. Then thank our heavenly Father for the love he pours out on our lives.

Love is kind.

Blessings of Each Season

*For everything there is a season, a time for every activity
under heaven.* Ecclesiastes 3:1

Each season brings its unique blessings. With summer heat
comes recreational fun. In autumn, brilliant landscapes
blaze with color. We celebrate Jesus' birth in the ice and
snow, and spring brings rebirth and resurrection.

Like each season of the year, each season of life is
special. We experience the growing up of spring, the high
activity of summer, the slowed pace of autumn, and the
wisdom of winter. We often fear the passing of time in our
short lives, but we can learn to appreciate the distinctiveness of each season.

By placing our hopes in the loving hands of God, we
can trust him for fulfillment. It is never too late for us to
have a significant life.

Choose today to accept where you are rather than
squander your resources trying to be what you're not.
There is beauty in each day, just as there is beauty in each
season. Allow yourself joy, and look for things to give
thanks for every day. In thanksgiving, we see God's blessings and grow closer to him.

God fulfills our lives.

Mud Pies and Mint Tea

Two people are better off than one, for they can help each other succeed. If one person falls, the other can reach out and help. But someone who falls alone is in real trouble.   Ecclesiastes 4:9-10

I treasure childhood memories of warm summer days spent with my brother and a few friends bike riding, making mud pies and mint tea, and catching crawfish with bologna bait. Carefree days and simple friendships can be beautiful parts of growing up.

Somewhere along the journey to adulthood, we lose pure friendship to middle-school identity crises and high-school popularity contests. In adulthood, true friendships can be befuddled by fears of rejection. The habit of replacing friendships with work, television, and anonymous Internet chats comes easily.

God uses events and circumstances to bring us together and reconnect us in friendship. God created us to need each other. Through the hug of a friend, a spouse, or our children, we experience the warmth of God's love. Through the positive words of our friends and family, we receive God's cheerful, supportive encouragement.

God blesses our lives with the gift of earthly friends.

Bless a relationship today.

Today's Gift

This is the day the LORD has made. We will rejoice and be glad in it.   Psalm 118:24

It happens every year at our house. Actually, every three months or so, we celebrate another birthday. Weeks of planning go into the party, and several children, each carrying colorful packages, descend upon our home to celebrate. There are party games and cake and ice cream, of course, but the real joy comes in the anticipation of the gifts. I love to watch the eyes of a child who is opening a brightly wrapped package!

Each day holds the promise and excitement of a beautifully wrapped present that is just for you. Often, we are focused on gifts that may await us in days to come, or we regret gifts that we left unopened in the past. It is easy to neglect this day that we have been given for discovery and enjoyment. Go ahead—pull the shiny curling ribbon, rip off the wrapping paper, and discover what lies inside!

We sometimes have a hard time knowing what someone else wants or needs, but God knows us better than we know ourselves. He knows the desires of our hearts, and he is waiting for us to open the gift of today.

Enjoy the gift of the present.

Brown Moth

We are citizens of heaven, where the Lord Jesus Christ lives. And we are eagerly waiting for him to return as our Savior. He will take our weak mortal bodies and change them into glorious bodies like his own.

Philippians 3:20-21

Have you ever seen a caterpillar and wondered what type of butterfly it would become? In our home, we witnessed a certain beautifully colored caterpillar throughout its transformation. We were expecting a butterfly, but to our chagrin, this caterpillar spun a moth-type web around itself. Sure enough, about two weeks later, a brown moth emerged from its silky cocoon with bulging eyes and ugly little wings. How could such a beautiful caterpillar transform itself into such an ugly moth?

In our world, we see flashy people and throngs of others wanting to be just like them. They seem beautiful on the outside. But for all of us, unless we trust our lives to Jesus' transforming love, we will not transform into the lasting beauty that new life in Jesus brings. Like the moth, our appeal will end quickly.

When Jesus transforms our hearts to be more and more like his day by day, we will experience life fully.

Let Jesus make your heart beautiful.

Meaningful Mentoring

The godly give good advice to their friends.

Proverbs 12:26

Because males dominate the engineering fields, Purdue University decided that female engineering students could use some help. As a sophomore in mechanical engineering, I participated in Purdue's experimental mentoring program. Without the supportive connections made within our mentoring framework, I would not have succeeded in that major.

When life gets rough and the going gets tough, wise people seek help, support, and advice from their friends. God gives us the privilege of sharing our life experiences to help others, and mentoring brings significance to our own success.

Choose a particular area in which you enjoy making a contribution, and volunteer your time to help others succeed. Whether it be reaching out to a less-experienced person in your vocation, volunteering at a local pregnancy-care center, or tutoring recent immigrants in an adult literacy program, make a commitment to help others with your time and expertise. Have lunch or coffee, and stay connected by offering your continued support. The gifts received on both ends of the mentoring effort will be priceless, and you will leave a significant legacy beyond your own life.

Seek out a mentoring relationship.

Seize the Daylilies!

The grass withers and the flowers fade. . . . And so it is with people.   Isaiah 40:7

Daylilies are almost impossible to destroy. They survive drought, winter cold, and summer heat, and they are among the most beautiful flowers in the garden. Daylilies get their name from the fact that their flowers last only one day. In the morning, the bud swells and opens, and it shrivels back to nothing by evening. Daylilies must be enjoyed each day, because they don't last any longer!

Perhaps from a heavenly perspective our lives on earth last no longer than the beautiful daylilies. Each day is a gift from God to be lived to the fullest! Enjoy each day and make the most of every opportunity. As the saying goes, dying is natural, but it is tragic not to have lived first.

From the daylily perspective, it seems futile to argue, fight, or fritter our days away. Many of us get to the end of our lives and wonder why we waited to live, why we didn't seize the days we were given.

Like the glorious daylilies, let us live our brief lives fully, love deeply, forgive willingly, and laugh a lot with those we love. Today is a gift to be enjoyed!

Treasure each day!

The Domino Effect

You can help those in need by working hard. You should remember the words of the Lord Jesus: "It is more blessed to give than to receive." Acts 20:35

Children love to play with dominoes—setting them up in closely spaced rows, pushing the first one, and watching the ripple effect as they fall. One little nudge makes quite an impact!

When we are empowered by God to make a ripple for him in the world, the effects are far reaching. Jesus spent time with God in prayer and quiet. He and the disciples really *lived* in the world. Jesus ministered to a hurting world and influenced it for the better, as God sent him to do.

We, too, are called to impact the world for Christ. Ask yourself what you have to give, and offer someone your time, love, and resources. As you surrender your efforts into God's hands, the ripple effect will make a big difference to others. There are opportunities to donate your time, skills, or money to poverty relief, for example— around the world or just down the street.

It is easy to come up with excuses. Instead, think of something you've always wanted to do, be radical, and do it!

Reach out to others.

Flowers in the Desert

Her desert will blossom like Eden, her barren wilderness like the garden of the LORD. Joy and gladness will be found there. Songs of thanksgiving will fill the air.

Isaiah 51:3

Imagine cracked, dusty earth. As you survey the desert wasteland, you discover a single flower standing alone, somehow defying the incredible odds against it by growing and blooming in the face of desolation.

Are you ever overwhelmed by the state of the world and your perceived powerlessness to change it for better? We become immobilized by the defeating odds against making a difference, but God wants us to take a stand and trust him for the results.

Just as a lonely flower in the desert blooms, fades, falls, and scatters seed so that more beauty can be created, God starts with something small and makes it grow beyond our expectations. Abraham lived as God's friend. He trusted God and took his stand despite his pervasively godless society. From the seeds of Abraham's faith grew a great spiritual heritage.

God controls all things, so take your stand! Go out of your comfort zone and invest your life for the benefit of others. The seeds of your beauty and love will nurture the spirits of many.

Bloom where you're planted.

Sum-Sum-Summertime!

We are merely moving shadows, and all our busy rushing ends in nothing.   Psalm 39:6

Ah! The joys of summer, with its warm sunshine, more leisurely pace, and hours by the pool! As soon as we busy women think about the lazy days of summer, we're on the phone scheduling all of those things that we think we have time for now that summer is here. Sports camps, music lessons, family reunions, a vacation here and visitors there . . . pretty soon our summers are chock-full of busyness and our lazy days have evaporated.

This summer, resist the urge to fill up all of your time. Take up things you long to do, and do them at a leisurely pace. Embark on a few creative, soul-refreshing projects. Learn a never-tried-before hobby. Plant a vegetable or flower garden and take time to sit back and enjoy it! Check out a few good books from the library with your children or grandchildren and read them together. Make a restaurant date with your spouse or loved ones. Plan a road trip with time for detours and spontaneous fun.

This summer, resist the temptation to fill in the empty calendar space. Relish some delightful unplanned days and enjoy this summer to the fullest.

Enjoy a simple summertime.

Sidewalk Ants

Let the children come to me. . . . For the Kingdom of God belongs to those who are like these children. . . . Anyone who doesn't receive the Kingdom of God like a child will never enter it.   Mark 10:14-15

As we buzz about, checking things off our lists, time keeps clicking on. It is easy to lose perspective. "Come on!" and "Hurry up!" are our endless refrains as we wait for our children, but perhaps stopping to watch the ants march through the sidewalk crack isn't such a bad idea.

What do we miss as we hurry through our lives? A leaf boat floating down the gutter, intricate snowflakes caught on black paper during a snowfall, the glistening dew lacing a spiderweb outside the back door—all of these are fascinating to children. As adults, we've lost our capacity for wonder, and thus we also lose meaning. As we ponder the ants underfoot, they teach us about God.

Jesus always welcomed little children. He never hurried them away in favor of more serious adult things. Instead, he corrected adults by telling them to be like children. Look at life through the eyes of a child today.

Cultivate wonder.

Cause for Celebration

Let the heavens be glad, and the earth rejoice! Let the sea and everything in it shout his praise! Let the fields and their crops burst out with joy! Let the trees of the forest rustle with praise before the L<small>ORD</small>. Psalm 96:11-13

There is a spirit of celebration in all of life—a cheery and colorful bouquet of flowers, a day at the beach, a campout with marshmallows by the fire, time spent gazing at a beautiful sunset. When we focus on ourselves and our problems, we shortchange our ability to celebrate. As we lift our problems and burdens into God's capable hands, we are able to experience the blessings and joy of our lives.

Each delicate, beautiful flower blooms in joy. Every majestic mountain rock praises our Creator. God's entire creation sings a symphony of his praises and gives him glory! We, too, can celebrate life by smiling at passersby, enjoying a relaxing dinner with loved ones, sending a card, or sharing words of encouragement.

Join the celebration of life today. Open your eyes to nature's beauty and allow the Lord to restore your soul. God's love and joy will refresh your mind and fill your day with rejoicing!

Always give thanks.

Redwood Grandeur

They are like trees planted along the riverbank, bearing fruit each season. Their leaves never wither, and they prosper in all they do.

Psalm 1:3

The natural beauty of the redwood forest captivates me. The sheer grandeur of age-old redwood trees inspires awe and creates a magnificent sense of how small I am in the presence of something so much greater. Lofty leaf work stretches skyward, scraping low clouds. The earthy evergreen fragrance draws me in, creating a calm peace and a sense of the richness of life.

It is difficult to imagine living as peacefully and richly as the majestic redwood tree. In keeping the pace of our performance-driven society, we find ourselves pushed to do more and more, to be stretched thin at the surface of our lives rather than living deeply and meaningfully. To live as peacefully and productively as the majestic redwoods, spend time nurturing the strong roots of loving relationships. Make a phone call, send an encouraging card, or say "I love you" to someone special in your life. Spend time in prayer, and read and apply God's Word. God's peace and blessing will soon fill your life.

Nourish the roots that support greater peace and joy.

Relationships enrich our lives.

Handful of Summer

You will enjoy the fruit of your labor. How joyful and prosperous you will be!   Psalm 128:2

Beyond our garden gate stands a patch of raspberries. We started it a few years ago from some pass-along plants. Each year, the raspberries enthusiastically extend their boundaries. One of our favorite experiences of summer is eating raspberries right off the vines and bringing in what is left for later. Raspberries mingle a delightfully tart and refreshing flavor with the joys of summer! We cherish them by the handful.

It is very satisfying to enjoy the fruits of our labor. Behind the rewards that we enjoy is a tremendous amount of hard work. Raspberries require planting, watering, staking, weeding, and picking—and encountering the raspberry thorns.

Every good thing in life—such as raising children—takes a lot of work. When we follow God's lead in obedience and perseverance, we receive the rewards that God gives to those who faithfully love and follow him. Serving others, remaining thankful during tough times, and deepening your daily relationship with God are difficult tasks that yield great rewards.

Despite the work and the thorns, cultivate the fruit that honors God. He will bless you with abundant joy and love.

Be fruitful and multiply your joy.

Slow-Growing Clematis

The Lord isn't really being slow about his promise, as some people think. No, he is being patient for your sake.
2 Peter 3:9

Clematis is a flowering garden vine that takes five years to really get established. Like trees, clematis is slow growing, but it is lovely to have in the garden. Gardeners always want it to grow faster than it does. A friend of mine planted lovely potted clematis last year, and this year she has seen no further growth. Our five-year-old clematis is quite charming, with its multicolored blooms that clamber up our arbors and peek through the climbing roses, but we have done a lot of waiting to get it this far.

The growth in our lives and in our relationships with God and with others doesn't happen overnight, either. We often expect unrealistically quick changes and growth in our era of microwaves and fast food. Growth, however, is a lifelong process.

Slow-growing changes are meant to teach us patience and faith, but we easily lose hope and grow impatient instead. Don't be discouraged! As we look back with some perspective, we can see that God has never stopped working.

God encourages our growth.

Water for the Wasteland

He found them in a desert land, in an empty, howling wasteland. He surrounded them and watched over them; he guarded them as he would guard his own eyes. Deuteronomy 32:10

It is late June, and already the grass is brown and leaves are falling from the trees. People run their sprinklers, trying to salvage the precious grass and pricey trees planted in this former farmland. The trees limp along, trying to survive until the next rain.

Our lives often resemble dry summer landscapes. We endure the heat of stress and busyness and the winds of demands and criticism. Without Jesus' life-giving water, our lives soon dry up and become wastelands.

We try to refresh ourselves in our own power. Diversions such as shopping, entertainment, television, movies, and busyness temporarily take our minds off our arid hearts. We limp along, barely surviving until the next quick fix.

Our deep needs for refreshment are satisfied only by the life-giving rain of God's grace and mercy. Whether in a torrent or by a slow, soaking drizzle, God showers his love upon us when we open our lives to his blessings.

Jesus brings new life.

Great Value

*How precious are your thoughts about me, O God. They
cannot be numbered!* Psalm 139:17

While strolling through the discount store recently, we
discovered some out-of-place plants. They were a much
sought-after type of ever-blooming hydrangea. Since it was
late in the planting season, the hydrangeas were severely
marked down—a bargain for those who knew their value!
Of course, we took one home and planted it in the shade
among our other hydrangeas.

If we just knew our real value, think of how our lives
would bloom! So often we calculate our worth according to the criticisms of others, believing that we just don't
measure up. On the contrary, our real value is only derived
from the One who created us. God says that he loves us,
and he shows us his love with many wonderful gifts.

God created humans so that he would have someone
to share the joy of living with, for life is always richer when
it is shared. The Creator of the universe knows our names
and how many hairs we have on our heads! We must be
incredibly valuable!

God knows our lives, with our mistakes and triumphs,
and loves us just the same. We have incredible value in
God's eyes!

God values you!

Drag or Adventure?

I am the LORD your God, who teaches you what is good for you and leads you along the paths you should follow. Isaiah 48:17

The joys of summer come in many forms. In the gardens, tall garden phlox releases a delicious fragrance into the breeze when it blooms. Beside this beauty, overlooked thistle weeds, scratchy and thorny, also grace our gardens.

The experience we have of our summer gardens depends on our perspective. We could see only the weeds—the stubborn thistles, plantain, and dandelions. Or we can choose to see the beauty instead of the weeds. Wherever there are things of beauty, there will also be undesirable elements. In this life, nothing is or ever will be perfect.

Our Lord knows each plan we make for our lives. He tells us that we should trust in his plans and rest the future in his hands. We can choose to see beauty in life through the lens of hope, or we can emphasize the weeds.

Life is either a drag or an adventure, depending on how you look at it. We face this choice every day. Despite the thorny weeds in our lives, we can fix our eyes on Jesus and choose the adventure of seeing beauty today.

God has great plans for us.

Avian Team

Make me truly happy by agreeing wholeheartedly with each other, loving one another, and working together with one mind and purpose. Philippians 2:2

Walking past the breakfast table one morning, I did a triple take out the window. Perched atop our pergola near the patio was a dog-size red-tailed hawk. Without hesitation, the boys and I ran outside, waving our arms and making a racket to shoo it away from the robins' eggs just below. As the hawk flew to the fence, we heard a great commotion. Every bird in the neighborhood was squawking. When the hawk flew to our neighbors' rooftop, we stood in amazement as the dive-bombing mockingbirds and robins attempted to drive the hawk away. Apparently, its dream of a robins'-egg breakfast wouldn't come true, thanks to the neighborhood bird team. When the hawk left, the neighborhood peace returned.

Just as saving the nest was a group effort by all of the neighborhood birds, so also we need each other in life. We were not created to go it alone, and we cannot withstand life's obstacles without the help and support of friends and neighbors. Get to know your neighbors and lend or accept a supportive hand.

United we prevail.

Splash!

The LORD directs the steps of the godly. He delights in every detail of their lives. Though they stumble, they will never fall, for the LORD holds them by the hand.

Psalm 37:23-24

"Come on! I've got you! Jump!" I say encouragingly. My little guy stands wide-eyed at the edge of the pool in tiny swim trunks as his three-year-old brain calculates the risks of jumping in. Somehow, it seems too far to jump into my arms. Minutes pass. Finally, standing so close that I am holding his hands, he decides to jump. Once he jumps, he never stops. Grinning, he jumps again. . . . Splash! And again!

In daily life, it is hard to trust God. The temperature of the water may not be shocking, but we still need to feel God's hands holding ours as we follow his lead. Our greatest reassurance in contemplating the risks of faith is found in remembering God's nature. God is God, forever the same. He is always loving, compassionate, and full of grace. Though we may stumble, God will never be out of reach of our fall.

God wants to be our constant companion. Just as I wanted my little one to enjoy the pool, God wants us to enjoy life's blessings.

What is needed is trust.

Face the Sun

The Sun of Righteousness will rise with healing in his wings.

Malachi 4:2

In the summer, the sunflowers stand tall. Their bright golden faces cheer the world as they turn continually toward the sun.

The fabric of our lives is characterized by the loose ends of unanswered questions. Many times we allow those loose ends to tie us in knots. At other times, our lives come unraveled. God wants us to know that the loose ends are all part of the plan that is gently unfolding in his hands.

To overcome our questions and doubts, we can take a lesson from the sunflower and turn our faces toward the sun. In turning toward the Son of Righteousness, we experience his healing and become more like him.

We can entrust our worries to God. As we hold things loosely, we have space in which to grow. When we are at peace with life's questions, we grow in trust. Our relationship with God is strengthened through the trials of our lives.

Each day, commit the worries of your life into the faithful hands of God. He will bring you life and peace as you turn daily toward his healing light.

Jesus mends life's loose ends.

Fireflies

*O Lord, our Lord, your majestic name fills the earth!
Your glory is higher than the heavens. . . . I look at the
night sky and see . . . the moon and the stars you set
in place.*   Psalm 8:1-3

Around twilight, the magical mystery of summertime comes
alive with the fireflies. Catching these lightning bugs is a
treasured summer evening pastime in many parts of the
country.

God created countless small wonders, and people often
say that God is in the details of life. It is hard to imagine a
practical purpose for lighting up the rear ends of harmless
garden insects, so God must hope that we will take whimsi-
cal pleasure in this fairyland illumination of the landscape.

In a meadow full of fireflies, the flashing dots of light
mirror the stars. Although we can never get our human
minds around God's greatness, the combination of the
small lights on earthly evenings with the great lights of
starry space gives us just a glimpse of his incredible power,
love, and greatness.

The God of the universe wants to be our friend. He
wants us to enjoy the little fireflies and the great stars, and
marvel at his greatness.

God made fireflies and stars.

Freedom from Criticism

I will walk in freedom.   Psalm 119:45

Criticism comes at us from all directions in daily life—from dissatisfied clients, unhappy families, disgruntled coworkers, and crabby neighbors. Giving and receiving disapproval seems to be a permanent part of our imperfect world. However, excessive criticism of ourselves or others is never healthy. We criticize others (even those we love the most) and put them down because they just don't measure up. Though criticism comes easily, is it healthy?

We would do well to forgo the trap of criticism and focus on one thought: God loves us just as we are. He does not criticize, but he hopes that we will return to the freedom of living in love.

Take a long, hard look in the mirror. Ask God's forgiveness for items that come to mind. As you recognize your sin and repent of it, know that God separates us from our sin as far as the east is from the west (see Psalm 103:12).

When you have experienced God's forgiveness and favor, extend the same grace to those around you. Accept others for who they are, in spite of their imperfections. God will make your life shine with love.

Choose love over criticism.

Freedom to Be Me

You saw me before I was born. Every day of my life was recorded in your book.   Psalm 139:16

God gives us many gifts, and one of the best is the freedom to be ourselves. The great news for you and me is that God made each of us as we are for a reason. He loves the way that he put each of us together, for we are each a unique and wonderful creation borne out of his great love for us. In Psalm 139, David recalls God's hand in his own creation: "You made all the delicate, inner parts of my body and knit me together in my mother's womb" (v. 13).

Today, thank God for your individuality and pray for the ability to live with authenticity and integrity. Jesus said, "My purpose is to give them a rich and satisfying life" (John 10:10). The life that Jesus brings begins right now, and it is eternal. It is abundantly richer and more fulfilling than any life we could imagine. Accept God's precious gift of today and live fully as the person he made you to be.

We are unique and precious individuals.

Freedom

Love your neighbor as yourself.   Mark 12:31

Just like no person is perfect, no country will ever be perfect, either. Our country will never be exactly the way we'd want it to be, but we can be thankful for the many freedoms it offers us. We enjoy the freedom to speak, dress, worship, learn, work, eat, travel, make decisions, fulfill dreams, have peace, and live pretty much as we please.

Countries around the world still face unimaginable oppression. We must remember to support and pray for those who are oppressed and do everything in our power to help them find a life that honors God.

Many of our nation's founders were wise and God centered. God created human beings as equal before him, regardless of looks, money, power, or status. Jesus said, "The LORD our God is the one and only LORD. And you must love the LORD your God with all your heart, all your soul, all your mind, and all your strength [and] . . . love your neighbor as yourself" (Mark 12:29-31).

It seems that out of love for God and our neighbors, we should extend to others the freedoms that we enjoy.

Jesus sets us free to love others.

The Lord Is Our Light

Your word is a lamp to guide my feet and a light for my path.   Psalm 119:105

There is something about a lighthouse that is incredibly calming. Maybe the light shining brightly on a weathered, rocky coastline allows our minds to rest, knowing that even in the darkest storms, the light will shine on.

And so it is with God. Even in life's most difficult conflicts, he will never leave us stranded. His light will always shine to show us the way.

In the voyage of life, sometimes the sea is fair and life goes on as usual. At other times, we are lost in a raging storm. God's light is still shining in the midst of it all. However far from God we may roam, when we seek him, his light will guide us back to rest, joy, peace, and life. He alone ensures our safety as he guides us homeward.

Similar to the gentle grasp of my small child's hand with my larger one, we can know the familiar feeling of being guided by our own loving heavenly Father. Today, let God's light dispel the fog in your life.

Follow God's light.

Giving Our All

Then a despised Samaritan came along, and when he saw the man, he felt compassion for him.   Luke 10:33

Most of us are familiar with the story of the Good Samaritan. A traveler was robbed, beaten, and left to die. A priest and a Temple assistant came by, saw the man, and passed at a distance. Finally, a Samaritan, a man of a race despised by Jews, cared for the man, helped him to an inn, and paid his bill. After telling this story, Jesus said, "Now go and do the same."

It is hard for us to find time and energy to care for ourselves or others. Like the men that passed on by, we often prioritize our actions according to how we expect to profit or benefit from them.

Jesus' standard of giving is illustrated by the Good Samaritan, who may have spent his grocery money and used up his vacation days to care for this injured man without expecting anything in return. God calls us to defy logic by following God's lead and trusting him to care for our needs as we give of our lives for others.

Joyfully give your all.

Joy Finds You

Shout with joy to the LORD, all the earth!   Psalm 100:1

Dawn is the time of day that I love the most. In the summer, as the sun casts its first yellow haze, the dew-covered garden begins to shine. If we dare to venture out on the wet, early-morning grass, we see that each blade of grass, leaf, and flower is lined with glimmering droplets. When the sun illuminates the sleepy world, we see the extravagant hand of our Creator. This God who paints the dawn in dazzling, diamond-like dew is the same God who loves to bless us, show us his miracles, and make our God-given dreams come true.

As I walk about the sunrise gardens with camera in hand, I discover many delightful little surprises. The red-and-white Double Delight rosebud unfurls its breathtaking beauty. Adorned in dewy jewels, it raises its praise to our Creator. The over-swelled bud of the frilled pink daylily bursts with color and shimmers with life. Our backyard hummingbird hovers in beauty and grace as he takes in the nectar and delicious fragrance of the magenta garden phlox.

Tender peace and happiness wait just beyond your back door. Let the joy of nature's miracles find you today.

Experience the joy of creation.

Maine Road Trip

No one can discover everything God is doing under the sun.   Ecclesiastes 8:17

We love to vacation in the Northeast during the summer. Maine is a favorite destination, with its beautiful, rocky coastline. Lobster is plentiful, lighthouses are common-place, and sleepy little fishing bays dot the coastline. On one summer visit, we explored the jagged coast, discovered picturesque oceanside villages, and slowed down to take them all in. One evening, we enjoyed lobster and blueberry pie in a little seaside restaurant at the end of the road. On our way back to civilization, a breathtaking sunset framed a dock and rowboat. God's serene artistry was memorable.

God created the world for our enjoyment. There is far more to see than any of us can absorb in a lifetime, but it is good for our spirits to change the scenery from time to time. God wants us to explore and discover the wonders of his creation, to care for our world, and to share in the joy of living with God and with others. Today, go out and discover the world that God made for you to enjoy!

Explore and enjoy God's world.

Sailing Regatta

Since we are surrounded by such a huge crowd of witnesses to the life of faith, let us strip off every weight that slows us down, especially the sin that so easily trips us up. And let us run with endurance the race God has set before us.
Hebrews 12:1

Some summer Sundays, we enjoy sailing as a family on Grandpa's boat. We enjoy poking along across the lake, accompanied by a gentle breeze. One such day, we were thrilled to be sailing near a weekend regatta. Far from our easy Sunday sail, the regatta boats rallied for the best wind and cornered the racing buoys with astounding skill and speed. As they followed the course and the wind's direction, their spinnakers billowed like giant white nets.

The author of Hebrews compares our spiritual lives to a race. In order to sail well, we must throw off any extra weight of fear and sin, unhealthy relationships, over-busyness, and addictions. When we leave cumbersome personal effects behind, we can hoist our sails in faith, forget fear, and trust the winds of the Holy Spirit to make us victorious on God's course for our lives.

Strip off whatever holds you back.

Bravery in Spite of Fear

If you keep quiet at a time like this, deliverance and relief for the Jews will arise from some other place. . . . Perhaps you were made queen for just such a time as this?
Esther 4:14

Esther, a Jewish orphan living with her cousin Mordecai, won King Xerxes' favor and became his queen. In time, the king issued a decree for all Jews to be destroyed. When Esther learned of the decree, she knew that she must enter the king's presence to beg for mercy.

Esther disregarded the law forbidding anyone to approach the king (the punishment was death). She trusted God, entered the inner courts, and was pardoned by the king, who was pleased to see her since God had softened his heart. Esther eventually asked for mercy for her people. Justice was done, and Esther and her people lived because she was brave even when her life was on the line.

When we are on God's side, we know that God works with us to accomplish his purposes. Bravery means doing what we have to do even when we are afraid. When we follow God's lead, we can give our best, put fear behind us, and trust God for the results.

God works with us.

Summer Storm Clouds

He will make your innocence radiate like the dawn, and the justice of your cause will shine like the noonday sun.   Psalm 37:6

One of the hard parts about living in the Midwest is being without the daily inspiration and grandeur of mountains. But in the summertime, we often see visions of snow-capped mountains in the billowy summer storm clouds.

Just as storms transform ordinary clouds into snow-capped mountains in the summertime, the Son transforms ordinary things into something extraordinary. Dazzling dew, free to anyone in the world, is more brilliant than all the splendor riches can buy when the sun shines through it.

God also loves to take simple, ordinary people, fill their lives with his light, and watch their beauty dazzle the world. Ordinary people can do extraordinary things for God.

In order for God to shine through our lives, we have to allow him to fill us to overflowing with his life, light, and love. As we become transparent and allow God to shine through us, we will be alight with his beauty. Let him design the pattern of your stained-glass life.

Let God make you extraordinary.

Signs to Look Up

Since you have been raised to new life with Christ, set your sights on the realities of heaven.   Colossians 3:1

On a recent summer road trip, we drove through many construction zones. We all had to laugh at the words on one orange construction sign: "Overhead Power Lines," with an arrow pointing upward. Apparently, busy construction workers sometimes forget that their large machinery may collide with power lines above them.

We laugh, but in our busyness, we very often forget to look up and remember where we are and what we are doing. We, too, need reminders to look up to God for guidance, to connect with him, and to offer our thanks regardless of the circumstances.

God knows that we need to connect with him to remember who we are, maintain proper perspective, and see our surroundings through heaven's eyes. When we lose perspective, we become susceptible to fear and doubt. When we remember to look up, we gain confidence in knowing that God is God, and that he alone is in control.

Hang an inspiring photo or a favorite verse in an eye-catching spot. When you start to become overwhelmed, remember to look up and see God.

Look up to God.

Five Little Loaves

Then Andrew, Simon Peter's brother, spoke up. "There's a young boy here with five barley loaves and two fish. But what good is that with this huge crowd?" John 6:8-9

Did you ever feel that the next grade would just be too hard? I remember feeling that I could never learn the next grade's math. When we learn addition, multiplication looks horrifying, yet somehow we make it!

Step by step, we meet each new challenge of our lives. We finish school, go to work, get married, and become a mom for the first time. These are all big steps in our lives.

Jesus faced the challenge of feeding five thousand hungry men (see John 6). When Jesus asked if anyone had food to share, a small boy with tremendous faith and courage offered his little lunch to Jesus. The disciples laughed, but Jesus knew that when we make our little offerings with faith and courage, God can do a whole lot with it! That day, the disciples ate their words. There was so much food left over from the boy's lunch that the scraps filled twelve baskets!

When we give Jesus our best, he turns it into something great!

Offer your best to Jesus.

A Looser Grip

Though you do not see him now, you trust him; and you rejoice with a glorious, inexpressible joy.   1 Peter 1:8

Losing things is part of life, whether it is our keys, a job, or a loved one. Sometimes these losses seem overwhelming. When we are focused on what we have lost or on what we *might* lose, we fearfully cling to what we still have. When we realize that God wants to provide for our needs and give us hope, we hold life with open hands, knowing that it is not under our control. We can trust and experience joy again.

Isn't it true that when we let things go—by daring to release control—we receive the most joy? If we could respond to circumstances with gentleness and trust, we could experience life to the fullest. When we turn our lives over to God and let him carry us in his hands, our hands are free to catch the joy God sends us each day. We can help a neighbor in need, or stop and pick some roses. With our eyes fixed on Jesus, we can live confidently and securely, knowing that he will take care of us.

God provides in his time.

Our Watering Can

Always be joyful. Never stop praying. Be thankful in all circumstances, for this is God's will for you who belong to Christ Jesus.   1 Thessalonians 5:16-18

One of the most used garden tools in many backyards is the watering can. Water is a source of life in the heat-driven summer, a necessary element for every living being.

God satisfies the thirsty and fills us up when we are empty. God is our source of life; he wants us to have peace and happiness, enjoyment and purpose. Yet often we forget the source of our lives and dry up like plants in the summer heat.

Even when we're busy, we can still remain connected with Jesus. First Thessalonians reminds us to be thankful and joyful always, as we connect with God in prayer. "Never stop praying" does not mean that we kneel quietly with our hands folded all day, but that we continually look to God for help even when we're busy. If we realize that God is in control, we can be joyful instead of miserable, and thankful instead of always wanting more. These are ways that God refuels us in our full schedules.

God desires for us to be at our best—and in the process, to enjoy the ride!

Stay connected with God.

Drawn to the Light

Now you have light from the Lord. So live as people of light!
Ephesians 5:8

As we look out our window on a summer evening, we see a fluttering of moths hovering around the porch light, seemingly captivated by the warm glow. In a similar fashion, a life that shines with Jesus' light draws other lives toward it. Like summertime bugs, we are naturally drawn to the light.

A joyful life is irrepressible. True, lasting joy that radiates from a sincere heart illuminates the surrounding world, making it a brighter place for others. By living joyfully, we illuminate the world around us. Christ is more effectively seen in one joyful life than in thousands of sermons, for the light of God's presence shines on the surrounding world.

Set your sights on God, and let his light shine through you to others. You are the light of the world, a light that can be seen for miles. Go and shine your light for God today!

Shine God's light on the world.

Plastic Beauty?

What are mere mortals that you should think about them, human beings that you should care for them? Yet you made them only a little lower than God and crowned them with glory and honor. Psalm 8:4-5

We love spending our summer days at the pool. The scent of sunscreen mingles with the sound of splashing water. At a recent visit to the pool, I noticed someone who just didn't fit in. Her tanned-beyond-recognition, surgically enhanced body, styled and sprayed hair, and heavy makeup stood out from the other swimmers.

Obsession with our appearance is never healthy, and however hard we try, we will never be perfect! Starvation, surgical enhancements, compulsive exercise, and continual self-evaluation keep us from the healthy, joyful life that our Creator intended for us.

In every aspect of life, balance is very important. Being overweight and being over-obsessed with weight are both harmful.

Take a new attitude toward your body. The Psalms say that God created each of us to be glorious, like him! When we have a balanced approach to diet, exercise, clothing, and makeup, and take our self-worth from God, we are able to retain the joy of living!

Our value comes from God!

Make the Most of Today!

This is the day of the Lord.　　　　　Jeremiah 46:10

It's amazing to look at the calendar—the summer is already half over! Time always ticks on by, without asking whether or not we're ready for the next day. Vacation plans, summer activities, family get-togethers, and constant demands on our lives make the summer pass quickly. Making the most of every opportunity makes the passing days rich.

Don't let today slip by. Make a memory. Be intentional. Do something that makes your heart sing. Eat dinner in the tree house with your kids. Take a leisurely stroll in a garden or along a lake. Share a hug and an "I love you" with a loved one. Plan a new experience.

Great days often include time to relax and recharge as well as to serve and contribute. Don't forget to take a few moments for yourself. Time invested in yourself will add new life to the rest of your relationships.

Tonight, don't just plop down on the couch with a microwave dinner in front of the television. With a little more effort, your evening could bring your day to life!

Live every moment!

Where Is the Joy?

Martha was distracted by the big dinner she was preparing. . . . The Lord said to her, "My dear Martha, you are worried and upset over all these details! There is only one thing worth being concerned about."

Luke 10:40-42

A woman asked how my friends and I could enjoy vacations. In all seriousness, she confided that vacations had never been fun for her or her family. Despite extravagant outings to beaches, mountains, theme parks, and cottages, she had missed one essential thing—relaxing.

Regardless of destination—the park down the street or the pampering palace by the sea—the purpose of getting away is to unwind, to let everything go and take a different pace. It is often hard to escape the lure of television, cell phones, planners, and the Internet in our wired, accessible world, but we must disconnect to find joy.

Jesus encountered a similar scenario with his friend Martha. Mary, Martha's sister, was enjoying her conversation with Jesus while Martha was consumed with the meal preparations. We can take Jesus' answer to heart, for we all become too wrapped up in our agendas.

Take it easy and set aside your usual routine. Find enjoyment in sharing joy, love, and connection with others.

Enjoy life!

A Life-Giving Spring

Jesus grew in wisdom and in stature and in favor with God and all the people.   Luke 2:52

Growth is an essential element in every healthy life. Growth happens best when we give of ourselves and learn from our lives by reflecting on our experiences. Hard times especially allow for growth, causing us to look to God for strength and gain confidence for tomorrow's challenges.

In life, we all must grow and change to stay healthy. Our physical growth stops at some point, but continued mental, spiritual, and social growth is essential to a balanced life. Even Jesus had to grow—physically, mentally, and socially—into the man he was to become.

If we stop growing, our lives become stagnant and stinky like an algae-filled pond, which suffers when no water comes in and no water flows out. When we allow new learning to flow into our lives and pour our lives out for others, our hearts become life-giving springs.

Allow God to transform your life as you continue growing into the person he made you to be.

Growth is part of life.

Enjoy Today!

So I concluded there is nothing better than to be happy and enjoy ourselves as long as we can. Ecclesiastes 3:12

In our lives, busyness speeds the days along and life often slips by unnoticed. Sometimes we even wish the time away so that we can get on to better things. Haven't we all caught ourselves saying, "I can't wait until the baby's out of diapers" or "After we retire . . ." or "Once the kids are in school . . ." or "After the kids are out of the house . . ."? Yikes!

Though it seems as if life will go on forever, it won't. Circumstances change, we age, friends move, kids grow up, and loved ones move away or pass on.

Today is an occasion for putting your best foot forward. Today is the day to be at your best. Today is the day to show your love to those placed in your life.

Make time to express appreciation to God and to others for their gifts and their presence in your life. Tomorrow, things are guaranteed to be different.

Seize life today, and live it fully. Today may be the only day we have. Make it count, and enjoy the gift we've been given.

Live your life to the fullest today.

Nature's Beauty

Praise the LORD, everything he has created. . . . Let all that I am praise the LORD.   Psalm 103:22

There is so much beauty around if we stop to see it. If we slow down, we experience the wondrous ways that God loves to touch our lives. He graces our ears with melodious wind chimes, the joy in a child's laughter, the soft rustle of tall summer grass, and the rhythmic crashing of salty waves. He touches our eyes with vibrant blooms, patterned flowers, and bright light. He wafts the crisp cool breeze, the fragrance of roses, and the salty scent of the seaside under our noses. He tickles our taste buds with icy snow, refreshing herbs, the tart taste of fresh raspberries, and juicy homegrown tomatoes. He gives our lives texture with fuzzy caterpillars, silky bunny fur, and the smooth skin of a baby. God delights our senses with the majesty of his creation.

When we touch the creation that God has made for our enjoyment, peace fills our souls and joy radiates from within us. Take a step outside and allow God to touch your life. He made it all just for you.

Enjoy nature today!

Beautiful Butterflies

O LORD, what a variety of things you have made! In wisdom you have made them all. The earth is full of your creatures. Psalm 104:24

One of my favorite low-maintenance gardens blooms at the back of our yard. Our butterfly garden features many blossoms that butterflies love. The garden began as a way to beautify our fence and screen part of our neighbor's yard. Now, our summer days are graced with the constant presence of beautiful butterflies.

If you want to try this in your yard, start with a butterfly bush (buddleia). Plant it toward the back of the garden, as it will be five feet tall and just as wide. Then plant a few pink or yellow butterfly flowers (asclepiad). Asclepiads are the only plants that the regal orange and black monarchs will lay their eggs on. Add a few golden black-eyed Susans (rudbeckia) and coneflowers (echinacea) in the middle. Fill in the foreground with catmint (nepeta), pincushion flowers (scabiosa) and purple sage (salvia nemorosa).

Within a season, you'll be enjoying a beautiful butterfly garden in your own backyard! In three years, the garden will be lush with blossoms. In experiencing the delicate wonders of nature's butterflies, you'll appreciate the beauty and joy of God's artistry.

God's creation brings joy.

Power in the Storm

He calmed the storm to a whisper and stilled the waves.
What a blessing was that stillness as he brought them
safely into harbor!   Psalm 107:29-30

Summer thunderstorms are common in our part of the country. Other places experience tornadoes, hurricanes, wildfires, and landslides. No region of the world avoids nature's fury.

It is startling to realize that the same Creator that flings lightning and thunder, wind and floods through his mighty fingertips is also the Creator of gentle flowers. The same hands that display such power also coax each budding flower into bloom!

In our lives, we always face storms of some kind—work, relationships, finances, wars, death. The storms of life are terrifying, but they challenge us to grow individually and in community. They offer us the choice to strengthen our relationships with God.

In the face of each storm, we can choose to grow in wisdom and character or to stagnate in storm-beaten misery. To grow, we must seek the support of trusted friends and family, who withhold judgment and love us generously.

Trust God's gentle power in the midst of your storms and seek the guidance of his loving hand.

God sends storms and flowers.

Snowcapped Mountains

You make springs pour water into the ravines, so streams gush down from the mountains. Psalm 104:10

There is overwhelming beauty in the heights of snow-capped mountains. Wildflower meadows, stunning rock formations, graceful wildlife, and white-water streams remind us of the unspoiled beauty God created for us to enjoy. The mountaintop offers a breathtaking perspective, a new lens through which to see our familiar world.

Similarly, as salt water licks our toes, the vast, unending ocean draws us in. The sand, the continuous motion of the waves, and gliding pelicans touch our lives with serenity and peace. No wonder so many of us seek vacations in the mountains or by the ocean. It is human nature to be drawn to something so much more powerful than our individual selves.

In the context of natural grandeur, we sense God's presence and power. Such beauty captures our hearts and nourishes our souls. Rhythmic force and crashing power cleanse the spirit and purify the heart.

When our eyes are on our Creator and his bountiful creation, his beauty touches us in an extraordinary way. Take up a new lens and enjoy the beauty God provides for our enjoyment.

In grandeur, we see God.

Bigger Dreams!

Let us rebuild the wall of Jerusalem and end this disgrace!
Nehemiah 2:17

In a time when a city without a wall was like a home without walls, Nehemiah was intent on rebuilding the damaged walls of Jerusalem. Despite overwhelming verbal and physical opposition, Nehemiah and his team rebuilt the walls in just fifty-two days! Nehemiah had a grand vision, acted upon it, and relied on God to supply the miracle.

God wants us to have big dreams. If our dreams don't require a miracle, they're just not big enough. Dream bigger!

God wants to help you become all that he intended you to be—which is greater than you can imagine! When we follow our big dreams, we know that success rests with God's power, not our own. When we're walking toward our big dreams, there are two sets of footprints—ours and God's.

Think of something you have always wanted to do. It may not happen immediately, but keep dreaming. Sometime, somehow, your biggest, boldest dreams will surface. When they do, give your dreams to God. Pray daily for God's leading and for providential circumstances. Don't be afraid when the time comes to realize your dreams, for God is with you all the way. Dream big!

Dreams should be God sized!

Spreading like a Weed

They . . . win the confidence of vulnerable women who are burdened with the guilt of sin and controlled by various desires. 2 Timothy 3:6

I've often heard about a plant called lithrum. In our gardens, we love lithrum, a spiky magenta-flowered plant passed along to us by neighbors. Apparently, lithrum has made a bad name for itself in wetter parts of the country. Though it never gets out of hand here, lithrum tops the list of noxious weeds that endanger native plants in wetlands. I had a hard time believing this until our July road trip took us across hundreds of miles of interstate wetlands smothered in lithrum. Seeing is believing.

In 2 Timothy, Paul writes to Timothy about vulnerable, weak-willed women. These terms make busy women uncomfortable. We like to be known as capable, competent, and poised—*anything* but vulnerable. Yet, given certain conditions, we become just that.

Where we plant ourselves dictates the attitudes and behaviors we will take on. Like staying on a diet in an "all you can eat" dessert buffet, it is nearly impossible to remain faultless when we place ourselves in unfavorable situations. Choose the conditions of your life carefully. Forgo the weeds, and grow strong and beautiful!

Seek positive environments.

Shelter in the Rain

*When doubts filled my mind, your comfort gave me
renewed hope and cheer.*   Psalm 94:19

Gordo, our resident hummingbird, sat perched on a dry
mandevilla twig all day because of a rainstorm. Sheltered by
a large leaf, with rain dripping all around, our little buddy
sat and sat, preening his feathers, flying to the feeder, and
coming back to clean his feathers again. Despite the rain,
he was preparing to fly high at the end of the storm.

How often we find ourselves caught in life's rainstorms!
We sometimes see them coming, as with the prolonged
pain of slowly losing a loved one. Other storms come
suddenly, with a pink slip from work, harsh words, a
broken relationship, or an accident. Regardless, life's rainstorms send us to seek shelter. We need a safe place to
reflect, be nurtured, and heal.

God wants to shelter us in the rainstorms. His comfort
is healing, nonjudgmental, and compassionate. The psalmist says, "You, O Lord, are a God of compassion and
mercy, slow to get angry and filled with unfailing love and
faithfulness" (Psalm 86:15). God will heal and refresh your
soggy spirit.

With God's help, times of healing can prepare you for
flying even higher after the storm.

Seek shelter in hard times.

Prepare for the Catch

He picked up five smooth stones from a stream and put them into his shepherd's bag. Then, armed only with his shepherd's staff and sling, he started across the valley to fight the Philistine. 1 Samuel 17:40

Fishing is like life—you never know what you'll get.

On a recent fishing trip to a nearby pond, we were missing one essential item: a bucket. Yes, a bucket is necessary if you actually expect to catch something. We expected at best to catch and throw back a bluegill, but our oldest caught a dinner-quality largemouth bass . . . and we didn't have a bucket!

Young David went into battle believing that with God's help, he could defeat the giant Goliath. David trusted God for the victory, although he was just using a sling and a stone. God has great things in mind for our lives when we trust him!

Greet each day with a great attitude. Choose joy, hope, and trust, even when the odds seem to be against you. We can trust because we know the consistent, generous character of our God.

Go into today with a great attitude, whatever the conditions of your life. Oh—and don't forget your bucket! You never know when you'll catch a big fish!

Expect success.

Are We There Yet?

God raised Jesus Christ from the dead. Now we live with great expectation, and we have a priceless inheritance . . . that is kept in heaven for you.

1 Peter 1:3-4

"Are we the-rrrrrr-re yet?" "When are we gonna *be* there?" These questions are familiar to parents traveling with children. Whether we're driving to the grocery store or flying cross-country, we all want to reach our destination faster. We also want to reach the goals of our hearts without delay.

In life, we often ask this question of God: Are we there yet? The goals always seem farther away than we thought, and life's journey is long and hard. It is important to keep our eyes on our goals and not to get caught up in the bumps along the way.

The Bible says that we can have great expectations for life because of Jesus' death and resurrection. We have a priceless inheritance awaiting us in heaven. We are assured that heaven will be greater than the most wonderful dream imaginable. Jesus is preparing a perfect destination to conclude our journey.

Are you heading in the direction of your hopes and dreams? Trust Jesus and be your authentic self as you journey toward your inheritance in heaven.

Your inheritance is in heaven.

Candlelight and Bubble Baths

Be still, and know that I am God!   Psalm 46:10

Free time. What free time? We rarely have time for free time. Yet if we put away the blaring distractions of television and other media, we might actually have some space . . . for free time. We all need quiet retreats, simple evenings, safe harbors of rest where we can go when we need healing and peace.

Connecting with God does not require formal rituals. Surprised? The psalmist writes of God's hopes that we will "be still, and know" that he is God. Bible reading, prayer, and meeting with other believers are important to our spiritual growth, but God hopes that we will also spend time in quiet reflection.

It is hard to hear God in our noisy world. Make a personal commitment to slow your schedule today. Create a window of time for healing quiet. Allow yourself the simple luxury of a bubble bath or time to sit in the garden by candlelight. Sometimes our bodies are so busy that our souls need time to catch up.

Free up time to live fully, love and laugh much, and enjoy the gift of today . . . in stillness.

Seek peace and stillness.

Time to Be

A peaceful heart leads to a healthy body.   Proverbs 14:30

In the push and pull of a busy life, I am often run ragged. I don't like being frazzled and harsh with others. When I don't have time to put myself together, collect my thoughts, and pray through my day, I feel inadequate and depleted. In the midst of our high-speed lives, we must make time for ourselves.

We cannot give effectively or live joyfully unless we regularly disengage for a while. We all need time to find ourselves, be ourselves, and regain perspective. By re-centering our day, we will find that our faithful God is leading us to joy and love.

Reflection is essential for slowing down and quieting the soul. As a pond only gives an accurate reflection on a windless day, we need a quiet setting that will truthfully reflect our lives. Reading and sitting quietly with God's Word will bring his light into the situation. When we are deeply centered, we are free to hear what God is saying and understand how he is guiding us.

Enjoy quiet time to soothe your spirit today. Set aside a small part of each day to nurture your soul.

Pursue peace.

Know Peace

May the LORD show you his favor and give you his peace.
                                                    Numbers 6:26

Across from our neighborhood is a large open field, still undeveloped and notable for its wild beauty. Some mornings at sunrise, a silvery mist appears over the meadow and disappears into the far-off trees. In the fall, the trees speak even further of beauty with their red, yellow, and orange leaves punctuating the mist. God created a beautiful, peaceful world.

A popular bumper sticker reads, "No God, no peace. Know God, know peace." It's true, isn't it? God wants us to find peace by knowing him. Just as we must open our eyes to see the beauty God places in our lives, we must surrender if we want to know God's peace. I am not peaceful when I manipulate or control others to have my way. Only by knowing God and surrendering to his love and intentions can I have true peace. When we seek God, he shows us his favor.

Know God; know peace.

Handling Opposition

God is pleased . . . when you do what you know is right and patiently endure unfair treatment.   1 Peter 2:19

Earlier, while I was outside, a sweet melodious song was followed by a flying yellow streak across the yard. This chirpy little ray of sunshine was a goldfinch that perched on the spiky purple liatris for a few fresh seeds. Preceding his meal, he belted out song after song of praise.

If only we could sing such praises as we go about our days! Life is not always as sweet as we would like it to be. We often feel drained when we encounter opposition. A jealous friend, critical parent, discouraging boss, or whining children all make it difficult to maintain a positive attitude and pursue God's plan for our lives.

Jesus endured incredible opposition. His parents, friends, and family never quite understood him. We can face unfair treatment as Jesus did—with patience and the knowledge that God is in control.

As we yield our problems to God's hands, we can relax. Surely God is able to influence our hearts and the hearts of others to bring about his plan for our good. We can trust him, and in turn offer up sweet songs of praise to the God who meets our every need.

Give your troubles to God.

More Joy, Less Pride

"God opposes the proud but favors the humble." So humble yourselves under the mighty power of God, and at the right time he will lift you up in honor.

1 Peter 5:5-6

One way to measure our spiritual and personal health is to notice how we react when a friend or colleague succeeds.

When something unexpected happens, we reveal our true hearts. Our pride surfaces when someone we compete with succeeds, and we usually react by trying to make ourselves look better. Pride is prejudiced and argumentative. It denies any fault, desires to be important, lashes out when wounded, and puts others down.

In the Bible, we see many instances of selfish pride: the Pharisees, Judas Iscariot, King Saul, Eve, and, of course, Satan. We all naturally look out for number one and soon fall into sin.

Peter says that God wants us to humble ourselves so he can lift us up. In humbling ourselves, we don't think less of ourselves, but we are more aware of others' well-being. Life's greatest joys are found in really caring about another, in building others up, and in truly celebrating another's success. Pray today for God's help in loosening the grip of pride.

Humility is being accountable to God.

Pulling Weeds

When the crop began to grow and produce grain, the weeds also grew. Matthew 13:26

August always means weeds growing in every open space in our gardens. Though it takes a lot of effort to remove weeds, the pruning, chopping, pulling, and grooming has to be done.

Jesus often used stories to explain hard-to-grasp concepts. One such parable is about weeds, which pop up in all of our lives. Just as they do in my gardens, weeds grow up in our souls right next to the traits we are trying to cultivate.

It is easy to think that we are the only ones struggling with a certain weed, but when we stand closer, we see it in others' lives as well. We are all imperfect. We all struggle with jealousy, gossip, impatience, and anger that we pull and re-pull and pull yet again during our lives.

When you begin to see a weedy mess in your life, try taking a few pulls. Prune, chop, pull, and groom until you feel more free and joyful. We cannot enjoy life fully until the weeds have been pulled. The freedom and beauty gained is worth the patience and hard work!

Remove the weeds from your life.

Discovering Beauty

The perfection of beauty, God shines in glorious radiance.
Psalm 50:2

Dew drops along the delicate edge of a flower, the graceful curve of an unfolding rose, the subtle flutter of marvelously painted butterfly wings—there are many summer beauties. The sun dries the dew drops and beetles ravage the rose petals, but there is much to be thankful for in each part of life.

To be able to see beauty is a gift from God. There is much in the world that is less than beautiful, but usually, mixed in with despair and the less-than-ideal, there is a breathtaking glimmer of hope.

Finding beauty is only possible when it is first present within. Recognizing beauty despite imperfections requires a hopeful heart and a watchful eye.

To cultivate beauty in your life and hope in your heart, begin each day with a prayer for those qualities. Look for goodness in spite of the bad things that happen. Watch for opportunities to encourage, smile, offer hope, and live in joy. Plant a flower, send a card, make an encouraging phone call, and find a reason to say thank you.

Discover the blessing of beauty and pass it along.

Beauty brings hope.

Specks and Logs

Why worry about a speck in your friend's eye when you have a log in your own?   Luke 6:41

Have you noticed that women are always fixing things? We learn tricks for getting strawberry juice out of shirts, peanut butter off of sticky faces, and basil sprigs out from between another person's teeth. We love to point out others' messes, don't we?

Jesus addressed this attitude when he talked about judging others: "How can you think of saying, 'Friend, let me help you get rid of that speck in your eye,' when you can't see past the log in your own eye? Hypocrite! First get rid of the log in your own eye; then you will see well enough to deal with the speck in your friend's eye" (Luke 6:42).

Jesus defended a woman who was caught in adultery (see John 8). To the crowd ready to stone her, he said, "Let the one who has never sinned throw the first stone!"

Jesus sets a high standard of love by accepting us just as we are. In the same way, we should be quick to accept others without blame or fault-finding. Spread love and acceptance, and experience the joy found in loving others.

Jesus accepts us.

Simple Contentment

True godliness with contentment is itself great wealth.

1 Timothy 6:6

When we were growing up, trophies and medals, ribbons and certificates lined our shelves and sat proudly on our dressers as monuments to our achievements. Now, trophies that were once so important lie unseen in jumbled boxes. A higher job title, a prestigious degree, a bigger house and fancier car, a prominent position in society—these are the trophies that occupy our current shelves. Sometimes, when we take a step back to see what our trophies are made of, we realize how futile it is to pursue them.

We must ask ourselves whether we can take any of these things with us when we die. Are the people we spend most of our time with going to sit beside our deathbed? Have we marked a place in our loved ones' hearts? What is of true value in life?

The most valuable things cannot be bought with money. To be content is to live fulfilled, and this comes from living in thankfulness for all that we've already been given.

Start your journey toward contentment today, and joy and fulfillment will follow. Lift up your eyes in thanksgiving to God for the life you've been given.

We rest content.

Thrill of Faith

Come and see what our God has done, what awesome miracles he performs for people!   Psalm 66:5

It is hard to venture out on water skis. We contemplate the risks and the benefits of holding onto a rope while being pulled by a speeding boat. Yet when we decide to risk the adventure, we gain the thrill of the ride.

A step of faith is always hard to take. Sometimes it is hard to see where the road goes, and it is difficult to venture into the unknown. It is tough to break out of our routines and our comfort zones, to get up off the couch and away from the norm. The large leaps of a life of faith keep us on the track of God's plan for our lives.

Thankfully, God knows the future and controls all things. The only possibility for peace on earth comes from leaving life's outcomes in God's trustworthy hands. As we trust, we are enabled to rest, and we are empowered to live with life's questions because we know who has the answers.

Take a step of faith and experience the thrill of the ride!

Jesus calls us into the unknown.

Little Joys

From where the sun rises to where it sets, you inspire shouts of joy.
Psalm 65:8

As the carefree days of summer come to an end, make a point this week to enjoy the little things. Bring out a blanket, throw it on the grass, and gaze up at the passing clouds. Rest in the cooling summer breeze, and feel the warmth of the sunshine on your face. Enjoy a Popsicle by the doorstep. Go for a bike ride or fly a kite in the park. Gather a bouquet of roadside wildflowers and set it on your table. Whatever you choose to do, make the most of the season, for it will soon be gone.

We can enjoy the beauty of the season, for God's hope, life, joy, and love are found in nature as well as in those we love and trust.

Grab hold of God's strong and loving hand and know that he walks beside you. He will enable you to make the most of the little things.

Enjoy the simple joys of summer.

Celebrating You!

They will become festivals of joy and celebration for the people.   Zechariah 8:19

Colored ribbons and carefully wrapped presents, streamers and blow horns, and cake and ice cream are all treasured parts of birthday celebrations. Whether the party is a little picnic in the backyard or a festival for hundreds, the act of celebrating brings us to life. We all enjoy a special occasion that says, "You're important!"

God appointed feasts and festivals for his people. Celebration is a discipline as well as a pleasure. Sometimes it is hard to celebrate, to make the effort to overcome our grief, sadness, or discouragement and enter into someone else's happiness.

The psalmist speaks of offering a sacrifice of praise. This acknowledges that our praise is an acceptable offering to God and that it can be costly to put aside our fears and worries to recognize a victory or celebrate a success. Celebrations raise the bar and make it harder to retreat into gloom and doubt.

Acknowledge specific victories, large or small—losing a few pounds, working for ten years, graduating, toilet training a child, or enjoying a friendship—and celebrate them today.

Celebrate life today!

Works of Repentance

Go and sin no more.　　　　　　　　　　John 8:11

Coming upstairs after an early morning workout, I noticed that the portion of breakfast sausage Tyler was saving for a snack had disappeared from the breakfast table.

Hmmm. . . . After asking all three boys about the missing sausage, I noticed that Jesse, our boxer, was lurking in the shadows. Aha! Mystery solved: The sausage had been stolen by our dog! When Jesse knows that she's done something wrong, she crouches low to the floor. Jesse had been caught, and she was very sorry.

Just as I accept Jesse and love her even when she has done something wrong, our heavenly Father accepts and loves us despite our mistakes. Just as I can love Jesse but dislike her behavior, God loves us but dislikes our poor decisions, bad attitudes, and destructive acts. Just as I forgive Jesse for her wrong and expect her not to do it again, God forgives and forgets our wrongs. He also expects us to "go and sin no more."

Coming clean with God entails changing our lives. Instead of staying on the same wrong path, ask for Jesus' help in making a change.

Take action after experiencing forgiveness.

Shine!

Commit everything you do to the LORD. Trust him, and he will help you. He will make your innocence radiate like the dawn, and the justice of your cause will shine like the noonday sun.   Psalm 37:5-6

Day-to-day life is hard. Appointments, commitments, carpools, work, family, and church fill our days. We bounce like pinballs from one place and activity to the next. It is easy to become exhausted from the rat race, and every so often, we need to slow down and rediscover the things that are most important.

When we try to do everything, we are stretched too thin and the results are mediocre. When we find our purpose and commit our precious time to the things that make us tick, we come alive. When we return to the things that matter most, peace fills our soul and joy radiates from within.

Connect your head with your heart today. Let yourself hear what your heart is saying about your dreams, the things you love to do, the people you love to be around, and the places you want to go. Your life will *shine* when you listen to your heart and do what you were made for.

Allow your life to shine!

A Happy Heart

A cheerful heart is good medicine.   Proverbs 17:22

According to recent medical studies, laughter and humor are great medicine for human ailments. They say that the more we laugh, the more natural healing can take place in our bodies. Children laugh many more times in one day than adults do. Perhaps we need to add more cheer to our days and get rid of worry!

The more we open ourselves to new possibilities, the more we'll find ourselves delighted by the options opening up in our lives. When we trust God with the daily details, we are able to relax and experience joy. The opportunities and serendipities God provides surpass our limited vision and expectations. Rushing things to fit our agenda often means settling for less than God intended for us. Resting in his loving will and waiting on his divine provision will free us to enjoy what he has already given us today.

Today, I need to live intentionally. I need to let go of where I think I should be going, and the worry that accompanies it, and head in God's direction.

Do something today that brings joy into your life!

Make room for joy!

The Heart of Joy

I have loved you even as the Father has loved me. . . .
When you obey my commandments, you remain in my
love. . . . I have told you these things so that . . . your joy
will overflow!
John 15:9-11

I love to paint—not paint-by-number, but with oils on canvas. Sometimes when I have finished a painting, I know that it doesn't quite reflect what I see in my heart, but I look at all of my creations with love, knowing they are a part of me.

God has created everything that exists, and humans are his masterpieces. When God looks at us, he sees billions of human creations—each of us unique, and each of us reflecting his image. When I, as a flawed human creator, look at my work, I know that neither it nor my heart will ever be perfect. When God looks at his handiwork, he knows that it is perfect because it reflects his perfect heart. He looks at each of us with love, knowing that we are a part of him.

Our Creator loves us, so we can be filled with joy today.

God loves you!

Preschool Wisdom

So now we can rejoice in our wonderful new relationship with God because our Lord Jesus Christ has made us friends of God.　　　Romans 5:11

Children can be precious and wise, perhaps because of their pure hearts and simple faith. One day, our son had been to his preschool's monthly chapel time with our pastor. As we drove home, he disclosed his newfound wisdom to me. "Mommy, do you know the reason that God made us? So that we would be his friends!" Incredible! My little four-year-old had summarized life's true meaning—the reason for our being put on this earth.

Throughout Scripture, God plainly reveals his deepest desire—to enjoy life with the people he created. The value God places on us—the men and women he created to be his companions—gives an entirely new meaning to our lives. God leaves us free to do as we please, but he wants us to love him with all of our hearts.

God desires our friendship. There are billions of people on earth, but he loves each of us as if we were the only one. In each new day and moment, he gives us an opportunity to deepen our love, trust, and faith in him.

We are God's friends.

Beauty in the Sunrise

People are like the grass. Their beauty fades as quickly as the flowers in a field. Isaiah 40:6

It is easy to hurry through each day, but today will never come again. Nothing in our lives will be exactly the same tomorrow as it is today. Our loved ones and our relationships will all be a little bit different. Our youthfulness will fade, our children will grow up, and our relationships will change. Life is too short to just let it speed by.

There are things to be thankful for every day. We can be so focused on ourselves, our schedules, or our importance that we miss the momentary joy of the sunrise or of a toddler's trusting smile. God uses such details to touch our days and say that he loves us. Today's circumstances may not be clear, but we can trust that they are taking us to where we need to be tomorrow.

Stop yourself in the course of today. Allow yourself to see the handiwork of the Master Artist. This scene will never come again in quite the same way. Soak it up, lift your heart in thankfulness to the source of life, and allow the joy of each moment to fill you.

Stop and notice today's beauty!

The Canyon

*You have made a wide path for my feet to keep them
from slipping.* Psalm 18:36

As we looked out over the scene below, the natural rock
formations were breathtaking. The canyon was huge! The
floor was a long way down, and the other side was a long
way off.

So often, the ruts of our lives grow into canyons. On
one side is the life we're living, and on the other, the life
we want to live.

Staying with the comfortable life we already know
means fearfully settling for less than we are made for.
Venturing out into the unknown is an act of faith.

Each new day brings its own opportunities for growth.
Our lives are more than the events of being born and
dying—our lives are composed of each day that we live in
between.

The Lord of the universe has grand plans for each of
our lives. As we trust him to direct us, we become more of
who he made us to be. God makes our paths wide enough
to keep us from slipping, and he unfailingly holds our
hand.

Take courage, and cross the canyon to the life you want
to live!

Trust God to lead you today!

Enjoy the Ride

The LORD is watching over your journey.   Judges 18:6

There was a time when families enjoyed taking Sunday drives. The destination was not the main goal; the purpose was to enjoy the time along the way. Today, Sunday drives aren't so popular. Why? Perhaps higher gasoline prices have taken the joy out of the weekly drives. Maybe our other choices for family entertainment seem better. Most likely, the explanation is that we're too busy making good time wherever we go.

Today's hurried lifestyle can be experienced at every traffic light. Everyone races through the yellow light to make good time in getting wherever they're going.

In our lives, we push ourselves full throttle to achieve. We multitask to check more things off the list. Our days are more about making good time getting to our various destinations than about catching the joys along the way.

The Lord oversees every detail of our lives and will guide every step of our journeys if we let him. Perhaps we could slow down and enjoy the journey every once in a while. Maybe we could learn to trust God's guidance instead of our own lead-footed driving.

Take your life on a little road trip and enjoy the stops along the way.

Enjoy the journey.

Filling in Faith

So she did as she was told . . . and she filled one after another. Soon every container was full to the brim!

2 Kings 4:5-6

A woman had only one small jug of oil between herself and starvation when God sent the prophet Elisha to help her. Elisha told her to gather as many containers as she could find. In this account of God's tender care and love for those who are faithful to him, God's provision was as large as the woman's faith and her willingness to obey.

Overcoming her doubts, the woman lived out her faith, gathering many empty jars, as Elisha had instructed. If the woman had faith enough to ask for only one jar, her blessing would have only been one jar of oil. If she had rounded up even more jars, God would have filled them with oil as well.

God is ready to provide for those who have come to the end of themselves and realize that their own struggles to get enough does not satisfy or fulfill. In faith, we ask God to provide for details that are beyond our control. As we work on our attitudes, relationships, and responsibilities, we can have total confidence—God always provides for our needs.

God provides what we need.

The Blessing of Assurance

Now all glory to God, who is able, through his mighty power at work within us, to accomplish infinitely more than we might ask or think.   Ephesians 3:20

The infants' game of peekaboo is popular worldwide. Babies need the game, apparently, to learn about object permanence. When a face disappears from baby's view, the person is still there, even though baby doesn't think so. The game teaches them to trust.

Worries steal our joy and drain our energy. Assurance is found in knowing that God knows every detail of our lives. When we believe in God's loving care, our anxiety decreases and joy prevails. Real security comes from knowing that our future is in God's capable hands. We need to trust God enough to risk surrendering our lives to his will.

Overcoming worry comes from knowing God's character. When you feel yourself slipping into worry and distrust, remember his promise: "You will keep in perfect peace all who trust in you" (Isaiah 26:3). Memorize such encouragements, and hang them on your mirror where you will see them. Your faith and joy will abound.

God is able to do much more than we could ask or imagine—we just need to let him.

Trust God to care for you.

Coffee and Friendship

Where two or three gather together as my followers,
I am there among them.   Matthew 18:20

Today, I have the privilege of writing at a local bakery/
café. Across the way, I see a group of women meeting for
Bible study over lunch. What a blessing such times can
be! Women need female friends, yet in today's world of
cell phones and e-mail, our opportunities for contact are
often limited by the impersonal convenience of electronic
communication.

In past generations, women depended on each other for
survival. They washed clothes, quilted, tended children,
and cooked over the fire together. With modern technol-
ogy, our days are more efficient, and we are more indepen-
dent and self-reliant.

Our lives are strengthened as they are sustained and
held accountable within our friendships. Jesus says that
where two or more are gathered in his name, there he is
also. What a powerful reality—that when we are together
in like-minded harmony, Jesus is present as well.

Invest in your friendships. Make time for gathering at
church, in groups, and over coffee. Such occasions bring a
satisfying richness to life.

Support your friends.

Free from Fear

"For I know the plans I have for you," says the LORD.
*"They are plans for good and not for disaster, to give
you a future and a hope."*
Jeremiah 29:11

Fearfulness burdens our lives. One day we're walking down
the street, minding our own business, and suddenly fear
reaches out and grabs us. Thoughts instantly race through
our minds: *Something's going to happen to . . .* or *Something
could happen to . . .* or *Someone might reject me for. . . .* We
grab hold of the thoughts that motivate our fear and cling
to them tightly.

Fear debilitates our lives. It's as if joy, carefree days, and
laughter have made a permanent migration to some other
land. When fear grips us, we cannot live the full life we
long for.

We can overcome fear only by knowing that Jesus, who
has our best interests at heart, is in complete control of
everything in the universe. We have to trust him. In the
same way that we trust the floor to hold us up with each
step, we must have faith that God will support us in the
steps of our lives.

God has our best in store.

The Illusion of Safety

We know that God causes everything to work together for the good of those who love God. Romans 8:28

As humans, we often try to protect ourselves from our fears by trusting in things that we can touch, see, and feel— money, fame, good deeds, relationships, intelligence. When we have a bank account full of money, a prestigious college degree, and a loyal following, we consider that we are safe. We have plenty to fall back on if something happens.

You may have heard the statement that safety is an illusion, and that is true. Safety is a figment of our imagination. The idea of safety is a pacifier for our fears—comfortable, but not guaranteed.

If the God who determines the change of the seasons and regulates the ebb and flow of the tides is the same God who holds our lives, then shouldn't we take the safe risk of trusting God in all that a day brings? The only safe place to be is right in the middle of God's will, for it is there that we are enabled to walk on water and trust him without fear.

Allow him to hold you, and experience true peace and joy.

Trust God with your life.

No Fear in the Fiery Furnace

Shadrach, Meshach, and Abednego stepped out of the fire. . . . Not a hair on their heads was singed, and their clothing was not scorched. Daniel 3:26-27

The idea of overcoming fear by trusting in God reminds me of a favorite Bible story from the book of Daniel.

Three young men, Shadrach, Meshach, and Abednego, lived in the time of King Nebuchadnezzar. The king commanded everyone to bow down and worship his idol, or they would be punished by being thrown into a fiery furnace. The idea of dying in a fire did not dissuade the three men from standing firm and trusting God. They refused to disobey God's law and worship an idol, so the king had them thrown into the fiery furnace.

The king and his company jumped up in amazement when they saw that the three heavily bound men were walking around in the roaring fire, unbound and accompanied by an angel. After calling them back out, and seeing they were unharmed, the king declared, "Praise to their God!"

Nothing can interrupt Christ's constant presence with us, and if Christ is always with us, then we can be secure and live without fear. We are freed to enjoy the gift of today!

We need not fear!

Pack-Mule Mom

Jesus said, "Come to me, all of you who are weary and carry heavy burdens, and I will give you rest."

Matthew 11:28

Jesus says that he will give us rest when we are weary and burdened. Many burdens come directly from worry, which weighs us down. Moms often feel like pack mules when they're loaded down with keys, coat, kids' coats, bags, diaper bag, drinks, snacks, field trip papers, and mail. This is like carrying our burdens instead of turning them over to God. We'd rather carry these things around with us—just to be safe—than to lay them in the large, capable hands of our heavenly Father.

The Bible tells us that God knows what we will ask for in prayer before we say it, and that he knows the number of hairs on our heads. Wouldn't it make sense to lay our heavy load of worries in our caring Father's lap? He will care for us better than we could imagine!

Stop loading up with worries like a much-burdened mule! Your load will be lighter and your day will be brighter when you are not weighed down with things that are out of your control. Free yourself up so that you can fully engage in the day!

Give your burdens to God.

Less Is More

He sat down . . . and said, "Whoever wants to be first must take last place and be the servant of everyone else." . . . Taking the child in his arms, he said to them, "Anyone who welcomes a little child like this on my behalf welcomes me."
Mark 9:35-37

Little girls love the color pink, glitter, tiaras, and plastic rhinestones, and even big girls love having beautiful things. However, in adulthood we discover that the emblems of social success are pretty empty. Even with a huge house, a fast new car, incredible furnishings, a fashionable wardrobe, excellent health, a perfect body, and a devoted husband and kids . . . *we would still feel dissatisfied.*

When we collapse into bed at the end of the day, we wonder what it is all for. In the chaos of achieving, we long for meaning, for focus, and for a simpler existence. Jesus confronted the disciples' discussions about who would be greatest. He took a child in his arms and set our human perspective straight: Lasting greatness is measured in being a servant to others.

Perhaps seeking more possessions less aggressively and actively pursuing servanthood would leave more room for living.

Make room for living.

The Goodness of God's Grace

Let all that I am praise the LORD; may I never forget the good things he does for me. He forgives all my sins and heals all my diseases. He redeems me from death and crowns me with love and tender mercies. He fills my life with good things.   Psalm 103:2-5

Grace is hard for humans to grasp. It is similar to a run-and-jump-in-your-arms welcome home that only children master (well, the dog comes close). Just as a child lavishly showers love, God rains down his love in a spectacular reality called *grace*. God never makes prerequisites for our receiving his love. Like a child's welcome-home hugs, God's grace is available when we ask for it.

God's grace is a resource that we can build our lives upon. We are forgiven, loved, and accepted for who we are. Amazing, isn't it?

Open yourself to God's gift of grace. He wants nothing more than your friendship. Ask your Savior to forgive you for your past, to walk with you into your future, and to enable you to enjoy this day.

Grace is God's unmerited favor.

A Rose by Its Fragrance

God is love, and all who live in love live in God, and God lives in them.
1 John 4:16

Walking through the garden at this time of year is a fragrant delight. Mounds of tall garden phlox perfume the breeze with their soft, sweet aroma. Many August blossoms contribute to the sweetness, but the roses always steal the show. After planting the most fragrant roses available from years past, our gardens are now filled with them. Even blindfolded, we would know our roses by their fragrance.

Our lives also have aromas. The Scriptures say that love characterizes the lives of those who follow Christ. Fragrant love should flow freely from our lives.

"If someone says, 'I love God,' but hates a Christian brother or sister, that person is a liar; for if we don't love people we can see, how can we love God, whom we cannot see?" (1 John 4:20). Evidently, our relationship with God is clearly revealed by the attitudes and relationships we estab-lish on earth.

Just as a rose can be recognized by its beautiful fragrance, the world around us can recognize our Savior because his love flows through our lives. Live in love today!

Loving lives are fragrant.

On His Shoulders

The people . . . are loved by the LORD and live in safety beside him. He surrounds them continuously and preserves them from every harm.   Deuteronomy 33:12

These dwindling, hot summer days inspire fun at the pool. Our boys are learning to swim like little frogs, darting about and splashing in the refreshing water. Soon they are worn out and ready for a rest, so we sling them on our backs and let them take a swimming piggyback ride on our shoulders.

God knows when we are weary and need a rest from the toil of life. "Let the beloved of the LORD rest secure in him, for he shields him all day long, and the one the LORD loves rests between his shoulders" (Deuteronomy 33:12, NIV). God loves to carry us on his shoulders!

Practically speaking, how do we find rest in our Lord? Our boys let us know when they are tired of swimming by asking for a ride. Then they climb on our backs and rest while we do the work. In the same way, we must ask God for a ride, then climb on his back for the rest we need.

Take a breather by riding on God's shoulders today.

God carries us on his shoulders.

Use the Good Stuff

We will bring the best of our flour and other grain offerings, the best of our fruit, and the best of our new wine and olive oil. Nehemiah 10:37

In the popular sitcom *Everybody Loves Raymond,* Raymond's parents always had their good sofa covered in thick plastic. The scene was funny because the sofa avoided being stained for forty years, but it was never really comfortable. In addition, their well-preserved sofa had become hideously out of style!

In life, things work better when we take time out for enjoyment. Who knows what tomorrow may bring? Think of all the "good" things we save for another day that end up never being used: china, the dining room, jewelry, towels reserved for guests, and the clothes that we save for a better occasion until they are outgrown or out of style. Women typically save many things for fear of ruining them.

God wants us to offer him our very best thanks, and he wants us to drink every single drop of the life he gives us. If we enjoy the things that we've been given, we'll surely gain much joy in return.

Enjoy using the "good" stuff today!

Offer your best to life.

Unsung Heroes

*Let everything you say be good and helpful, so that
your words will be an encouragement to those who
hear them.*

Ephesians 4:29

Our culture regularly sings the praises of celebrities. It is
natural to look up to others and to use their lives as inspiration for our own. However, the fascination sometimes goes
too far, and celebrities are often glorified without represent-
ing much that is praiseworthy.

In contrast, consider the unsung heroes who really do
inspire good qualities, who work hard and receive little
appreciation in return. A husband provides a steady income
for his family. A single mom balances many responsibilities to keep her family afloat. Firefighters, police officers,
and military personnel protect the freedoms we enjoy.
Schoolteachers prepare our future leaders despite daily
disrespect. Moms of newborns and toddlers are sleep
deprived, military wives keep their families together while
their husbands fight, and retired folk invest their wisdom
in younger generations. There are unsung heroes in every
walk of life who are honorable role models.

Encourage people you know who sacrifice for others.
Show them your appreciation in small acts of kindness and
love.

Encourage unsung heroes!

Labor of Love

She carefully watches everything in her household and suffers nothing from laziness. Her children stand and bless her. Her husband praises her.   Proverbs 31:27-28

Just the other day, I was thinking about the endless responsibilities of women's lives, especially the lives of moms. Just when we've checked a task off of our to-do lists, it is time to start over again. After cleaning up the kitchen from breakfast, we're bombarded by the lunch mess. After folding the weekly nine loads of laundry, we start washing, sorting, folding, and putting the same laundry away all over again. There is not much that actually remains accomplished. The minutes-ago clean window is resmeared with paw, finger, and nose prints. Not much is done that doesn't have to be redone.

A beautiful chapter of the Bible extols the virtues of a woman of character. "Who can find a virtuous and capable wife? She is more precious than rubies" (Proverbs 31:10). God values women who are excellent wives and mothers, and who achieve amazing things outside their homes.

In the midst of our repetitive daily tasks, we can look to Proverbs 31 for inspiration. In the composite character exemplified there, we learn how to live a joyful, rich, and blessed life.

Loving lives are praiseworthy!

For the Big Boss

Work willingly at whatever you do, as though you were working for the Lord rather than for people.

Colossians 3:23

I remember starting my first job. It was great—until reality set in! Lifeguarding was a great way to earn a paycheck, but it required hard work, such as mopping, testing the water, and cleaning the pool, even when dirty diapers exploded. Yes, work always turns out to be work, however much fun we think it will be.

Since Creation, God has given humans work to do. Whether it be teaching math, sorting information, caring for children, performing surgery, or calculating rocket science, work uses our God-given abilities to contribute to society—and, of course, to earn a paycheck.

God suggests that we work as if he were our boss. In any work situation, we choose to work with a good attitude or a not-so-good one. Certainly no boss is perfect, but Jesus is! He knows how hard we work and sees the attitudes of our hearts.

When we choose to be thankful to God for the opportunities he provides, we will have a cheerful heart at work! Work as if God were your boss, and you will experience joy and satisfaction.

Work cheerfully as unto the Lord.

Memorable Mistakes

So be careful how you live. Don't live like fools, but like those who are wise.   Ephesians 5:15

Mistakes are things we wish we had never done, times when we wish we had a "do over" button, and situations that we hope will soon fade from memory. My life includes many such mistakes. One occurred when our three boys were under four years of age and I was preparing dinner. I put our taco shells in the oven to broil for a minute, but I set the oven too high and didn't start the timer. I then made two much-needed diaper changes and read a few pages from a picture book. Soon smoke rolled across the kitchen and flames leaped out of the oven. A big mistake—and I haven't attempted taco shells since!

Whether it is a diaper thrown in the washer with the laundry or a missed bill payment, we often make some kind of foolish mistake. They tend to happen as we try to be superwomen, multitasking and committing to too many things. With our minds going in twenty different directions, we make mistakes.

Mistakes help us grow and learn to avoid similar situations, but we would do well to wise up and slow down a little.

Wise up and slow down!

Parallel Forgiveness

And forgive us our sins, as we have forgiven those who sin against us.

Matthew 6:12

Life is too short to be lived without forgiveness. We often offend others, and we are often offended by them. Since none of us are perfect, our lives are guaranteed to be battered by hurts, but we don't have to let them steal our joy. If we learn to let hurts go, we can know the freedom of forgiveness.

In the Lord's Prayer, Jesus says that God's forgiveness parallels our forgiveness of others. If we forgive readily, knowing that others are no more perfect than we are, then God will also readily forgive our sins. Until we forgive others, God will not forgive us.

Lack of forgiveness brings a heavy burden of anger, distrust, bitterness, and a growing grudge. To live and not forgive is to not live at all.

True forgiveness occurs when we pray the same blessings on those who have hurt us as we ask for ourselves. In other words, we know we have forgiven someone when we hope the best for them; it begins when we stop trying to get even.

Wipe off the scowl of past offenses and begin to let them go.

Be forgiving.

Over Your Head

No eye has seen, no ear has heard, and no mind has imagined what God has prepared for those who love him.
1 Corinthians 2:9

Most of us dislike feeling overwhelmed, yet all of us get in over our heads once in a while. We come up gasping for air as though we have been in the deep end of the pool for too long.

The life that God hopes we will choose will take us out of our comfort zones. We step up to the plate wondering if we'll even hit the ball, while God has visions of home runs and grand slams. When we are equipped by God and his Holy Spirit, we don't have to rely on our own strength.

How do we respond in the moments of opportunity God provides? Do we draw on his power? God has much greater things in mind for our lives than we could imagine. We need to trust in his power and walk through the doors he opens.

In fulfilling God's plan, we often find ourselves in over our heads. When we know that we are doing something incredible, we know that God is working through us, and we experience incredible joy!

God has big plans for you!

Maintaining an Image

My purpose is to give them a rich and satisfying life.

John 10:10

Recently, a news documentary covered an interesting story about one of our current heads of state at the White House. Apparently, reporters and photographers scrutinize her every move. Looking for a moment of weakness, these photographers caught her wiping her brow with her hand, and depicted her as being worried and overburdened from a single uncharacteristic photo.

It is exhausting to maintain a certain image while being watched and criticized for every tiny flaw. We often try to cover up who we really are for fear that others will not like our true selves.

We need to be brave and stop trying to please everyone else. Instead, we need to express our true values, enjoy life, and love without always worrying about how others will react.

Take a stand! Lighten up and have confidence in who you are! You were made to bring God glory by being the person he made you to be. Invest your time in those who accept you as you are. You can't live in a mold. Jesus came to make your life rich, satisfying, and joyful. Trust Jesus and be the person he made you to be!

Jesus broke the mold.

Rocky Mountain Grandeur

There you saw how the LORD your God carried you, as a father carries his son, all the way you went until you reached this place. Deuteronomy 1:31, NIV

Short on breath and muscle weary, we were having a hard time on this high-altitude trail. We hadn't expected snowy slopes and icy fields at the end of summer. We were over halfway up to Emerald Lake in the Rockies, the youngest of the five of us not yet three years old.

"Me tired, Daddy."

"Yes, we're tired too."

We knew the view ahead would be worth the sore muscles and the extra hike—and it was breathtaking.

The journey of life sometimes seems too hard, the obstacles too many, and the incline too steep. It seems that God is leading us on a road that just gets harder without reaching the rewarding view. In Deuteronomy, Moses recounted the way that God carried the Israelites through the desert and into the Promised Land. Moses encouraged his people and reminded them that though the journey might get tough again, God had promised to stay beside them.

Our destination in life will have a better view. Trust God, and allow him to carry you when you are weary.

God carries us through hard times.

Cleaning Out Clutter

Jesus told him, "I am the way, the truth, and the life."

John 14:6

One of my least favorite jobs around the house is cleaning the shower. Okay—it is definitely my most dreaded chore. Our shower ledge gets cluttered so quickly, and before we know it, it is collecting more grime.

In light of our culture's quest for "more, more, more," our lives are filled to the brim with too many commitments and cluttered with too many things. Often we are too busy to enjoy life. How can we steer our lives back to a joyful track?

We can start by simplifying. Like the stuff in the shower, our lives need to be sorted and cleaned. When we take inventory of the things that we love and feel inspired to do, and remove all of the things that burden us, we will be freer to enjoy life.

In order to live simply, we must continually clean out our lives, evaluate the clutter, filter the noise, and scrub the grime until we reach the gleaming white experience of a simple life—a life to be enjoyed, following Jesus.

A simple life brings freedom.

Into God's Hands

The LORD says: Do not be afraid! Don't be discouraged by this mighty army, for the battle is not yours, but God's.
2 Chronicles 20:15

Life is often uneventful and consistent, but we all have those memorable days when life hits a brick wall. There is unexpected news, unwelcome disappointment, or an unanticipated financial setback.

We all experience crises and tragedies. None of us are spared agony, grief, hardship, or trial. We feel lost and alone in the face of the unexpected, but we can rest in thankfulness for God's presence and peace.

Second Chronicles recounts an inspiring story about the nation of Israel. Disaster loomed as several enemy nations joined forces to attack them. Instead of responding with despair, Israel asked God to help them, which focused them on his power and not their own. God answered, "You will not even need to fight. Take your positions; then stand still and watch the LORD's victory. He is with you" (2 Chronicles 20:17). With God's help, Israel triumphed.

We can claim those same promises. In our struggles, pressures, and temptations, we can turn each battle over to God and be freed to praise and worship him. The all-powerful One will turn our sorrow into gladness.

God fights for us.

Struggling

With your unfailing love you lead the people you have redeemed. In your might, you guide them to your sacred home.
Exodus 15:13

Some days, our feet hit the floor on the wrong side of the bed, and we start the day with a bad attitude. It is easy to become stressed even before the day starts, allowing our frustration to pull our joy down. Pushing through our days burdened with fear, moodiness, and discontent leaves us exhausted—we miss out on the day's blessings and push others away.

When we try to control everything, we gain stress and lose joy. When we struggle to have things our own way and fight the current that would return us to joy, we become overwhelmed and exhausted.

This is not how God intends for us to live. Life was made for more than hardship. We can stop trying so hard and become the people God made us to be.

To enjoy each day he has given us, we need to release control and let God be God in our lives. In addition, we can choose to change our attitudes for the better. Only then can we let go of fear and discontent and experience life's peace and joy.

Struggles can turn to joy.

Let Life Come

I am leaving you with a gift—peace of mind and heart.

John 14:27

Let today come. The whole feel of the words seems contrary
to our get-it-all-done-now culture. However, letting the
day come seems to be how Jesus approached each day that
he spent on earth.

Jesus let God orchestrate the details of his life. He went
about his ministry with joy and love. Jesus didn't worry
about where he would stay or how he would be fed. He
didn't shout, rush, or impress others with his heavenly
credentials. Jesus rested in the hands of his Father, lived each
day fully, loved those around him, and anticipated his death.
He enjoyed the gift of the present.

It is so easy to worry about tomorrow or yesterday, and so
natural to try to impress those around us by competing and
comparing, that we fail to enjoy the life we can live today
with Christ's help. Success in God's eyes means becoming
the distinctive, unique individual God wants us to be.

Take it all down a few notches. Let life come as it was
meant to, and *enjoy* the journey of life!

Savor each experience today.

Across the Pasture

The LORD must wait for you to come to him so he can show you his love and compassion. Isaiah 30:18

On a recent field trip, our son's class stood at the edge of a cow pasture. The farmer let out one short, loud, "Sewwwweeeeee!" After about fifteen seconds of silence, we realized that the whole herd of cows had heard the call and were galloping full speed across the great stretch of grass—right for us! Reflecting back, I thought about myself and my own willingness to obey my Master.

Unlike the cows, I don't always come running. I find myself answering the call by thinking that I am really comfortable in this nice, cozy place eating grass and lying beneath this little shade tree. I weigh whether or not obeying him will be worth the effort.

On this earthly side of the pasture, looking up at God, it is very hard to see what he has in store, but he always has our well-being in mind. Coming when he calls will be worth our sprint across the grass, because our Lord delights in showing us his love!

Listen to where God is leading you today—it will be toward greater joy.

God shows us his love.

Finding True Friendship

This is my command: Love each other.   John 15:17

Friendship is one of God's greatest gifts. True friends share our joys and our burdens. They help us to grow and to see our lives from another perspective. Friends celebrate life with us in all its splendor and walk with us when the going is tough.

Do you want to experience friendship in its purest form? Practice the following and you will build great relationships:

Put others first and serve them wholeheartedly.

Forgive and let go. No one is perfect. God moves on despite our blunders, so we can move past our hurts and live in joy!

Invest time in your most important relationships. Many people will want to be on the receiving end of your giving spirit, but choose to invest in relationships that also nurture you in return.

Serve with a joyful spirit. A warm smile goes a long way.

At all times, have a thankful heart. People love to be appreciated.

Pray for your friends. God wants to bless you with the gift of friendship. Thank our Lord for the incredible gift of a friend who brings joy to life!

True friends are life-giving!

Authentic Beauty

I will brighten the darkness before them and smooth out the road ahead of them.   Isaiah 42:16

As the leaves begin their slow change into autumn colors, we appreciate the brilliance God brings to each autumn. The turning leaves reveal their true colors. The green camouflage that trees wear in spring and summer just covers them until they can reveal their authentic beauty of brilliant autumn oranges, yellows, reds, and burgundies.

Authenticity is beautiful. Just as the true colors of changing leaves bring incredible beauty to fall landscapes, the true colors of our lives are beautiful.

The meager life we mustered before we met Jesus is pale in comparison to the abundant life he brings. The soothing spring and summer greens are like our safe, comfortable lives before we turned toward God. Life in relationship with Jesus is far more brilliant and exciting than just existing for ourselves.

Even in its autumn splendor, the color of a tree's leaves is distinctive. Many trees, such as the sunset maple, are named for the color their leaves turn in the fall. We, too, are invited to show the distinctiveness of our true colors.

God promises to guide us in our authentic walk with him.

Be yourself!

Blessings Poured Out

"Bring all the tithes. . . . If you do," says the LORD . . . , "I will open the windows of heaven for you. I will pour out a blessing so great you won't have enough room to take it in! Try it! Put me to the test!" Malachi 3:10

Fall is when we celebrate the harvest. Farmers gather seeds and plant them, then turn their work over to God. The miraculous provision of crops all depends upon God's supplying rain, sun, and good soil, and sprouting, growing, and sustaining the crops until the last grain is weighed. Farmers supply a lot of labor and a whole lot more faith.

God loves it when we come to him in faith. When things aren't within our control, we have to count on him to provide the miracle. Despite our natural distrust, we can choose to give.

God wants us to offer him our best, with enthusiasm and thanks. Everything we have belongs to God. Just as the farmer supplies the faith and God supplies the crops, we need to trust God to supply our needs. As we do, God will abundantly pour heaven's blessings into our lives.

When we give, we receive.

Colors of Creation

Like the light of morning at sunrise, like a morning without clouds, like the gleaming of the sun on new grass after rain.
2 Samuel 23:4

Imagine a world without color. What a bland world it would be! Fortunately, God, the Great Artist, loves excitement and spice, beauty and delight. In the act of Creation, he invented infinite variations of beauty—in rainbows and sunsets, butterflies and ocean colors, morning light and intricate flowers—and he includes us in his beautiful creation! Each rising and setting sun displays his great artistry for everyone to see.

Like a well-written symphony, various garden elements come in and out with their interludes and melodies, each with its own color, texture, and vibrancy, to combine as an exquisitely whole, beautiful composition. How much richer our world is for the various arts that enrich our existence and carry our senses and perceptions to a higher level! How much beauty there is around us, if we can open ourselves to see it! All of nature's beauty around us is God's artwork, made for us to discover and enjoy. Appreciation for God's beauty heals the soul.

Today, experience God's touch in the thousands of reds painted into one flower.

Open your eyes to wonder!

Offering Our Best

Be sure to give to the LORD the best portions of the gifts given to you.
                                                    Numbers 18:29

Bathrobes and sweatpants, junk food and media entertainment make it easy to compromise our best for what is comfortable. It is much easier to e-mail than to send an old-fashioned handwritten note. It is easier to flip the channels on a remote than to flip the pages of an engaging book. It is easier to grab a bag of preservative-laden snack food than to plan a fresh, healthy meal. It is certainly easier to throw on loose sweatpants than to look our best.

Making the more comfortable, time-crunched choice is like using a paper bag instead of smooth silk. The ordinary brown paper is dry and rough, and it tears under stress. Living at our best, we assume the beautiful and serene quality of silk. God does not want paper-bag lives for us. Instead, he hopes that we will put our hopeful hearts into our daily lives.

It is tragic to be living without really being alive. Commit to becoming a better version of yourself today than you were yesterday. Exercise, eat well, and engage in life with those you love. Read, learn, and grow. Find joy in living each day fully!

Be fully alive—thrive!

Ending Summer

I will watch quietly from my dwelling place—as quietly as the heat rises on a summer day, or as the morning dew forms during the harvest.   Isaiah 18:4

Although the kids are back in school and the pools are closed for the season, our calendars still say that it is summer . . . for about two more days. As the beauty and fullness of summer fade, the season of autumn bravely approaches. This time of year is sad as we bid farewell to copious gardens, dazzling butterflies, and endearing hummingbirds. The coming of autumn signals change. In our becoming-chilly Midwest, we begin to hunker down for the long months.

God has made every season for a purpose. Solomon wrote, "For everything there is a season, a time for every activity under heaven . . . a time to plant and a time to harvest. . . . God has made everything beautiful for its own time" (Ecclesiastes 3:1-2, 11).

God delights in creation, and in our delighting in his creation. The key to living in God's peace is in realizing, accepting, and giving ourselves to God's purpose for our lives. God watches over us and makes all things beautiful in his time.

Autumn brings new beauty.

Miraculous Migration

Is it your wisdom that makes the hawk soar and spread its wings toward the south?   Job 39:26

The regally dressed, tangerine-colored monarchs miraculously migrate every autumn. If you look, you may see monarch after monarch fluttering through traffic, gliding over fields, stopping to refuel from the last flowers, and heading on south. Every year, they winter-over in regions of Mexico, California, and a few other warm parts of the United States. Scientists have not found any explanation for their repeated routes.

Though summer monarchs live for only a few weeks (migrating monarchs live through migration and the winter), successive monarch generations have been proven to fly the same family routes year after year. They all return to the same overwintering tree groves after journeying hundreds of miles. God looks after the butterflies' well-being and gives them the wisdom and endurance to fly and avoid frost. What a wondrous God we have!

Just as God keeps birds and butterflies on the right path, he points our own lives in the direction of our true home. When we seek God and his will for our lives, we gain his wisdom, and it guides our way.

Trust God and his guidance for your life today!

God directs birds, butterflies, and you.

Awakening to Life

What is important is faith expressing itself in love.

Galatians 5:6

Looking across the nearby meadow, I experience a canvas of God's splendor. The autumn patchwork of changing leaves in the forest beyond the meadow is breathtaking. Some autumn mornings are accompanied by a silvery mist that lingers over the meadow and conceals the turning leaves beyond.

The days of our lives are like the turning of the autumn leaves. Each day, we turn more toward God, or turn further away from him. We do this in each little choice that we make, even in issues that seem insignificant and unrelated to our relationship with God.

In turning more towards God, we choose faith, and we express that faith through love. Serving others and making life more about others than about ourselves is a great expression of love that can be found in turning toward God.

What legacy would you like to leave? How can you begin? Dig deep and listen to your heart for ways that you would love to give.

Point yourself in the direction of loving service to others, and you will come to life. Make your life count for something beyond your own earthly existence. Turn toward God and be fully alive!

Make your life count.

Choosing Joy

We were filled with laughter, and we sang for joy. And the other nations said, "What amazing things the LORD has done for them." Yes, the LORD has done amazing things for us! What joy!
Psalm 126:2-3

A few years ago, I realized that I so often concocted expectations for future events that I was rarely able to live in the present, much less enjoy it. It would be easy to postpone today's opportunities until Joey is out of diapers or until we finally have enough money. It is hard to see today for what it is—the only day we have. We're so busy thinking of what tomorrow might bring that we forget to enjoy what is happening right now!

Happiness and joy in our days are not determined by circumstances, but by how we choose to interpret them. We can be aware of the blessings we have lavishly been given by God beyond our deserving. Or we can think of the things we don't have yet but think we deserve. Some people choose joy, and some don't.

Our attitudes will determine whether or not joy comes into our days. Open your eyes to the beauty of the changing leaves in the autumn world. Choose to enjoy this day!

Choose joy today!

Pressed Leaves

We are all infected and impure with sin. When we display our righteous deeds, they are nothing but filthy rags. Like autumn leaves, we wither and fall. Isaiah 64:6

Recently, I opened a favorite book, and several flat brown leaves came tumbling out. I remembered the expressions of love represented by the vibrant red leaves given to me by our boys. The eager smiles and hugs they offered with their red leaves were treasures in themselves. The dry brown leaves now hold little of the sentiment from that day.

Many times we try to save things in life. My pressed leaves are dull, lifeless, crackled, and browning around the edges.

Sometimes we live as though we're trying to save life up for a better day. We have good intentions, but will that better day ever come? Today was meant to be lived fully! All too soon, our lives, like the autumn leaves, will wither and fall away. Thank God for his gift of Jesus' sacrifice, which allows us to choose Jesus and live!

Take up and live the life God has given you, with your eyes wide open. The brilliance of life will linger if we open our hearts to the joy of each day.

Live in joy today!

Love Clearly

Now we see things imperfectly as in a cloudy mirror, but then we will see everything with perfect clarity. All that I know now is partial and incomplete, but then I will know everything completely, just as God now knows me completely.   1 Corinthians 13:12

Near our home is a pretty little pond surrounded by myriad shades of green willows, reeds, and grasses. The pond is busy with quacking mallards and the V-shaped formations of flying geese. By fall, the pond is cloudy and gives little reflection.

The same cloudy effect can appear in our lives. Children see life through clearer lenses and purer hearts. Adults tend to be clouded by the confusing world and have more trouble reflecting Christ's joy and love.

We will experience a lens change when we see Jesus in heaven. All the obscurities of living in a dark world will be brought into his light. Everything hindering our sight will be taken away, and we will clearly see the light of our great God.

Even on earth, we can experience Jesus' light in our lives. He will bring us out of the fog, make our way clear, dispel our fears and darkness, and allow our lives to reflect his great love, joy, and peace.

Come into Jesus' light.

Invitation to Joy

You have turned my mourning into joyful dancing. You have taken away my clothes of mourning and clothed me with joy, that I might sing praises to you and not be silent. Psalm 30:11-12

We occasionally receive e-mail forwards, and the underlying message of some of these e-mails is disturbing. A recent one ended, "You can't become a Christian by attending church." *Hmmm . . . ,* I thought, *definitely not an encouraging word!* The whole e-mail used condemning scare tactics.

Sometimes we are confused about how to share our faith with others. Many people try to show others that what they are doing is wrong, and that "Christians" do things right. Such influences lay a guilt trip and scare people away. Guilt and condemnation are not from God.

Nehemiah said, "The joy of the LORD is your strength!" (Nehemiah 8:10). When we live in joy, others are naturally drawn to us as Jesus shines in our lives.

What could be better than sharing our joy about the difference Jesus has made in our lives? He turns our mourning into dancing!

Invite another to joy today!

Our joy comes from Jesus.

Skipping Rocks

God's purpose was that we . . . who . . . trust in Christ would bring praise and glory to God.   Ephesians 1:12

I love standing on stones at the edge of a body of water. There is something cool, pure, and consoling about both rocks and water. Skipping a smooth stone across the water is quite a thrill! "One . . . two . . . three," we count as the stones hop over the still water. As each stone touches the water's smooth surface, the water ripples outward.

In the daily grind of life, most of us focus on income. How much we make has a big effect on what we do with our days, but God's plans are not restricted by money. Instead of focusing on income, we could focus on what kind of impact our lives are making. God's purpose for our lives is not to earn more money, but to bring him praise.

God has given you a gift. Believe, discover, develop, and cherish it. Use it and give it away. Make an impact!

Skip your stones out onto the water and allow your life to make some ripples. Live to make a difference!

Make a difference!

Red River Gorge

The LORD says, "I will guide you along the best pathway for your life. I will advise you and watch over you."

Psalm 32:8

We love to go exploring. There is nothing like wild, unknown territory. One autumn, we explored the Red River Gorge, hiking the trails and taking in its incredible natural beauty. Another trail promised views from a natural bridge, but we encountered multiple paths while climbing the trail. Without signs pointing the right direction to our destination, we would have ended up elsewhere. Of course, the view from the bridge was spectacular!

Much of our lives, when we dare to venture out of our comfort zones, are spent exploring. We know our desired destination and try to find our way there. The Lord guides us along the best paths for our lives and watches over our steps as we go.

When our way is uncertain and the world seems to fall apart, we can rest on God's promises. He will show us the way, but we have to step out by choosing trust over fear and faith over worry. The view from the top will be breathtaking!

Trust and follow God's signs.

Shaped and Formed

O LORD, you are our Father. We are the clay, and you are the potter. We all are formed by your hand.

Isaiah 64:8

I fondly remember seventh-grade art class, when I first stepped up to a potter's wheel. A bit unsure about the gooey clay, I hesitantly put my lump on the wheel. Once the wheel started spinning, I loved it. The clay was soft and easily formed by my hands, but it had to be centered and balanced on the wheel for the form to emerge. Each slight touch of my fingers impressed a new shape on the spinning clay.

Isaiah writes that our Father, the Creator of the universe, forms us by hand. We begin our lives without much shape, and over time, God transforms us more and more into his image.

God gently shapes our lives. As the Artist, he knows what shape he would like our lives to take. As our world spins on his potter's wheel, he allows circumstances and events to caress our form. He works his love into our lives, and keeps them in balance on his wheel. God shapes our beings into glorious works of art that reflect the heart of the Potter.

We are shaped by God's hands.

More Precious Than Rubies

How precious are your thoughts about me, O God. They cannot be numbered!   Psalm 139:17

As we go through life, it is easy to feel depleted. Busy schedules drain our time and energy, and life begins to pull us down. Just as a beach ball at the swimming pool cannot stay underwater for long before it pops back up, those held by God in daily life cannot stay under for long. Though life takes us down, God lifts us up by his love and gives us value.

David describes God's deep love and constant thoughts about each life he has created. "O LORD, you have examined my heart and know everything about me. You know when I sit down or stand up. You know my thoughts even when I'm far away" (Psalm 139:1-2). There is no time when God is not thinking of each one of us.

Our Creator is captivated by us—he loves the way he made us.

Regardless of what lies in the past, God wants a relationship with you for the future. Trust your God-given value. Take the first step toward becoming the woman he made you to be.

God gives us great value.

Hide-and-Seek

I could ask the darkness to hide me and the light around me to become night—but even in darkness I cannot hide from you. Psalm 139:11-12

At this time of year, the neighborhood children take advantage of the shorter evenings to play hide-and-seek by flashlight. All through the twilight hours, flashlight beams dance and weave, as the person who is "it" seeks the hiders. Then we hear the familiar "I found you!"

Just like us, God feels that shared experiences are sweeter than being alone. God created each of us to share our life's experiences with him. Though God gives us free choice, he hopes that we will choose to love him. Each day, we can go our own way or live in God's company. He loves us so much that he gives us the choice.

All of life brings fresh opportunities to choose God. Wherever we go, God pursues us. If we hide, God can find us, even in the dark. He knows our thoughts and our plans.

Allow yourself to be found by God today, and live in the knowledge of his love. It is richer than we could imagine.

God keeps looking for us.

All Made-Up

You made all the delicate, inner parts of my body and knit me together in my mother's womb. Thank you for making me so wonderfully complex! Your workmanship is marvelous—how well I know it. Psalm 139:13-14

Little girls like to play with makeup. Lip gloss, eye shadow, and nail polish are to them what chocolate is to grown women. The feeling of becoming more grown up and beautiful is powerful. No matter who we are or what we look like, all women long to be beautiful. We hope to be desired, discovered, pursued, and loved, even when the makeup comes off.

It is healthy to want to be beautiful. The Bible tells us that God made us all in his image. He loves us and knows each of us completely—and he loves the way that he made us. To know his complete love for you and me is the first step toward healthy self-acceptance and worth.

A healthy body and a radiant smile bring so much beauty into our lives. Take steps toward becoming healthier, inside and out. Take a walk, prepare a fresh meal, read a book, spend time in reflective silence, have coffee with a friend, eat dinner as a family, and discover the naturally beautiful you!

God created our beauty!

Inward Beauty

The LORD said to Samuel, "Don't judge by his appearance or height. . . . The LORD doesn't see things the way you see them. People judge by outward appearance, but the LORD looks at the heart."   1 Samuel 16:7

Our nation is known for its emphasis on outward beauty, fashion, youthfulness, and thinness. Advertisements promise a smaller dress size, vanishing wrinkles, cute clothes, and better hair. Few advertisements promote an improved interior like a more loving heart or a more serene soul, yet our exterior always reflects our inner life.

The Lord explained his divine perspective to Samuel, reminding him that he looks at our hearts. A more glamorous exterior doesn't impress God. He loves us for what is inside, and for how our lives manifest the fruit of the Spirit. When we have his Spirit within us, we will exhibit "love, joy, peace, patience, kindness, goodness, faithfulness, gentleness, and self-control" (Galatians 5:22-23).

In Matthew 6:22, Jesus said that our eyes are the lamps of our bodies. Our eyes shine the light that comes from our hearts. The radiant beauty that shines from a heart filled with Jesus' love is reflected in our outward appearance.

Discover the true beauty of sparkling eyes and a shining smile.

Beauty comes from within.

The Setting Sun

Search me, O God, and know my heart. . . . Point out anything in me that offends you, and lead me along the path of everlasting life.   Psalm 139:23-24

I love to watch the sun setting in the evening sky as it casts its golden-bronze light on the world. The contrasting shadows appear bluer and longer, especially during the autumn.

The sun that so beautifully illuminates the natural world is the same light that exaggerates the crumbs on our floors and the grime on our windows. When God's light comes into our lives, it exposes our hearts' filth and clutter.

We can draw the blinds and shut the doors of our hearts to God's revealing presence, but we would miss out on the cleansing truth of God's love and the beauty of a life lived for him. We have to be willing to expose our imperfections to the light and allow God to free us from them. Only then will we live freely, knowing that we are forgiven and set free to be who God made us to be.

God's light reveals our hearts.

Sunset's Golden Glow

The Word gave life to everything that was created, and his life brought light to everyone.   John 1:4

As I write, the roses are blooming extravagantly, as if to shout their last hurrah before their long winter's rest. The setting sun lights each blossom. The colors seem richer somehow, as each graceful curve of bud and petal is beautifully defined by golden sunlight and blue-toned shadows.

Our colors become richer as Jesus' light shines through our lives. A life fully surrendered to God becomes a stained-glass window—more beautiful with the light shining through it. He lights up our lives with the unmistakable glow of his presence. Yet even with God in control of our lives, we still are not perfect. Though we surrender control of our lives to God, we still make mistakes. Jesus uses those broken pieces to form a pattern that will reflect his light.

The truth is plain and simple . . . and incredibly freeing. God wants to bring true light and life into our days. He wants us to live freely, able to enjoy each day with love and laughter. God's glory is fully revealed in a joyful life.

God's light shines through us.

Stepping-Stones

The LORD always keeps his promises; he is gracious in all he does.   Psalm 145:13

The cool water of the autumn stream passes by, carrying brightly colored leaf boats to their resting places downstream. The fallen leaves spin gently as they drift past my stepping-stones.

God prepares a path for us through life, step-by-step. He always calls us on to the next step; as we stretch our toes toward following his lead, God presents the next stone to step on. God never lets us remain long on the stone of the status quo. He continually challenges us to grow. He stretches our hearts to make more room for him, and he enables our love to overflow into other lives. With each step, we become more like Jesus. As we say yes to his leading, God equips us for what comes next.

When we must cross an impossible stretch of life, our powerful God guides and secures our way. God keeps his promises. He will never let us down, and he will always provide for us.

In searching for our purpose in life, we will find that the only lasting fulfillment comes from following our faithful God across the stepping-stones that he provides.

Follow God's path.

Crispy Leaves

Anyone who does not remain in me is thrown away . . .
[and is] gathered into a pile to be burned.   John 15:6

The yards behind us are well shaded in summer by several
old ash trees, so in autumn, the ground is covered with
fallen leaves. Those leaves, now lifeless, are raked into piles
to be burned.

Our daily schedules tend to exhaust and frustrate us.
Like the crunchy brown leaves, we become separated from
our life source and lose our vitality. We experience forgetfulness, moodiness, sleeplessness, divisiveness, and mean-
inglessness. Such symptoms warn us to take a step back
and realize that we are doing too much.

God hears us and meets us where we are. He gently
helps us to move from striving to trusting, from doing to
being, from pushing to resting. Our Lord God wants us to
have a more abundant, less hassled life.

The key to refreshment and productivity is reconnec-
tion with our source of life. Unless we are held in God's
hands, we become withered and crispy like the fallen
autumn leaves. When connected to him, we experience
contentment and joy. Rest and enjoy God's full life today.

Slow down and rest.

Like Treasure

Don't you realize that your body is the temple of the Holy Spirit . . .? You do not belong to yourself, for God bought you with a high price. So you must honor God with your body. 1 Corinthians 6:19-20

Within nearly every home around the globe is a receptacle for unwanted household items. Our kitchen garbage can is full of discarded wrappers, containers, and junk mail. Every home also has a special place for household treasures. Whether they are jewelry, photographs, memorabilia, or rocks, treasures are carefully kept in their best condition.

We can easily distinguish trash from treasure by the way we treat it. Trash is haphazardly tossed and discarded; treasures are gently handled and carefully placed.

The way we treat our bodies shows how we regard them. We often mistreat them without even thinking about it, but God clearly says that our bodies are his temples, and that we should honor him with them. Instead of mistreating them, we should keep our bodies in top condition by not smoking or indulging in other harmful habits. We should maintain a healthy weight, exercise to stay fit, and resolve emotional and social conflicts. Invest energy in caring for your body today.

Your body is the Lord's temple.

Fall Is for Planting

So let's not get tired of doing what is good. At just the right time we will reap a harvest of blessing if we don't give up.
Galatians 6:9

Every spring, I love the cheery beauty of daffodils and tulips. To have tulips, however, Midwest gardeners usually plant a new batch every year. Just as the best time to plant a tree was the previous year, the best time to plant tulips is autumn. Tulips require a lot of work, as each bulb is planted six inches deep. The more work we do in autumn, the more beautiful the display will be in the spring.

Just as we reap a large harvest from our planting, hard work in daily life will yield rewards. The best time to start spending time with God, saving and storing up the riches of his wisdom, is today.

Let your dreams and visions affect your planning for the future. No time, you say? Saving 15 minutes each day by streamlining your routine and 15 more by avoiding distractions will earn you an extra 125 hours per year. Watching 30 minutes less television per day would yield an additional 125 hours to invest toward your dreams and visions. Begin today!

Plant tomorrow's harvest today.

Piles of Leaves

One day some parents brought their little children to Jesus so he could touch and bless them. . . . Then Jesus called for the children and said to the disciples, "Let the children come to me. Don't stop them! For the Kingdom of God belongs to those who are like these children."
Luke 18:15-16

On a recent autumn day, I had many errands to run. Thankfully, I had my hurried perspective rearranged a bit that day. Our neighbor with the big trees had been raking leaves into enormous, inviting piles. As we were getting ready to leave, our neighbor called and invited us to play in their leaves. What three energetic boys could pass that up?

After an exhilarating morning of jumping in the crunchy leaves, my perspective was restored by enjoying the gentle wonders of life. Sometimes the blessings may seem small, but noticing the miraculous beauty of each day brings us back to the things that matter most.

Jesus agreed that we need a childlike perspective. He said that God's Kingdom belongs to those who are like children. We can live each day, starting today, in God's Kingdom by having the perspective of a child. Allow yourself time to regain the joy and wonder of the autumn season.

Rearrange your perspective!

For Love

Let us continue to love one another, for love comes from God. Anyone who loves is a child of God and knows God. 1 John 4:7

We all have something that we do simply because we love it, even though it may seem crazy to others. For some, this love happens to be skydiving or running marathons or helping out in homeless shelters. And though others may think that we're nuts, we do these things because we *love* them.

We encounter love every day—crazy love for a child needing care through a sleepless night or selfless love for our spouse and family. Love is beautiful, generous, and joyful.

Jesus said, "There is no greater love than to lay down one's life for one's friends" (John 15:13). We are to give ourselves for others just as Jesus gave his life for ours. Love is beyond logic or emotion. It requires a gut-level decision to give beyond reason.

On this earth, to love is to make an impression, to leave a mark of our lives on that of another. Today, love by giving encouragement, and by listening, helping, and giving. Love given away will return to you a thousandfold in joy, purpose, and meaning.

Lovingly give of yourself.

Make a Memory

To me, living means living for Christ.   Philippians 1:21

One day, we're experiencing the joy of welcoming our child into the world, basking in one of life's great miracles. Before we know it, our little bundle of joy is all grown up! It always seems too soon for losing the first tooth or riding a two-wheeler, much less earning a driver's license or going to college. Being a parent is a process of letting go from that first moment, and the years fly by very quickly.

As moms, grandmas, aunts, and mentors, God has given each of us a role to play in the lives of our little ones. Give the gifts of time and acceptance. Striving for power, prestige, and money may bring immediate gratification, but investing our lives for the benefit of our children is priceless and eternal.

The greatest glory we can give to God is to give our lives away in love for others. Plan something special—a game night or a cookie-making night together. Show your little ones how special they are. Get on their level and appreciate their interests. Look into their eyes and tell them how much you love them.

Love your little ones!

Chrysanthemum Dazzle

Each time he said, "My grace is all you need. My power works best in weakness."　　　2 Corinthians 12:9

To cover the bare front gardens, I planted a few lovely chrysanthemums to liven up the fall landscape. Mums never become the stars of the garden, but some mornings, adorned in dew dazzled by the rising sun, they can be incredibly beautiful. God can also make our ordinary lives shine for him. Sometimes the beauty comes from God's light shining on our tears.

Just as a flower blooms extravagantly on each day of its short life, we were created to live each day in full bloom. Decide to look and feel your best today. Resolve to sleep well and to care for yourself. Simplify your schedule and spend some time doing things that you love. Make space in your busy day to spend time with God, for he will refresh you and bring joy into your day.

God will bring peace and joy into the lives of all who will let him. Don't be embarrassed about taking small steps. He will ask of you only what he knows you can handle. Step out in faith, and God will be with you!

God will help us.

Pumpkin Patch

The way of the godly leads to life.   Proverbs 12:28

A few years back, standing at the local home and garden store's seed display, our family decided to try growing pumpkins. We brought our seeds home, chose a little plot, and planted the seeds. Soon, a few shoots began to grow, and one day, a big yellow flower appeared. Our pumpkins were on their way! If I thought the flower was big, I was completely unprepared for the size of the pumpkin vine, which eventually took up the whole side of our house! Drastic measures were required to control the pumpkin's spread—it was taking over our neighbor's yard, too!

In long sleeves and pants, I pruned back the vines to a much smaller size. In the end, the pumpkin-growing experience was well worth it—each of our boys had a home-grown pumpkin for Halloween.

Sometimes there are situations and relationships that begin to take control of our lives. It is great to have people who care, but at times we have to set boundaries in order for our relationships to remain healthy. By carefully setting up guidelines and knowing our limits, we regain balance in our lives. Relationships within healthy boundaries bear life-giving fruit.

Set boundaries to gain freedom.

Fiery Sunset

Sing a new song to the LORD! Sing his praises from the ends of the earth! . . . Let the whole world glorify the LORD; let it sing his praise. Isaiah 42:10-12

Fall days bring scenes of fiery reds, oranges, burgundies, and yellows, as the turning leaves are touched by the low autumn sun. In the crisp autumn air, each leaf slowly twirls down amid a blaze of rich color. Today's azure sky is a backdrop to feathery clouds and puffed-up jet trails. As evening settles, color infuses each feather and puff of cloud with neon yellow, orange, and pink against the fading, powdery blue sky. The intense colors drain from God's painting into charcoal-sketched clouds against the darkening sky. At last, light emerges in the solitary brilliance of the evening's first star.

God uses everything, including sunsets, for his divine plan. It doesn't matter if we're five years old, fifty, or a hundred—God has a wonderful, unique purpose for each of our lives. We shouldn't be afraid to let God use us, for this will bring us great joy. Take a risk and make yourself available to God—and do what you were made for.

Our singing souls glorify God.

Blue Skies

The LORD told Gideon, "With these 300 men I will rescue you and give you victory over the Midianites. Send all the others home."

Judges 7:7

There is no blue like that of the crisp autumn sky. The rustling breeze pushes puffy white clouds across the silken sky, caressing the colored leaves as they gently spin to the ground.

God's love falls on us like autumn leaves. Some days, a sunny sky shows his beauty. On other days, we experience God's mighty power in a tough situation. We like to feel comfortable and in control, but God often displays his love, direction, and power in situations outside of our comfort zones. Gideon, whom God called to rescue Israel, experienced one such uncomfortable situation.

God surprisingly pared Gideon's army down to three hundred men, while the enemy had tens of thousands. To fight the pivotal battle, God instructed the Israelites to take up rams' horns and clay jars instead of weapons, and brought them the promised victory in a most unusual manner.

Life always brings hardships and impossible situations. When we look to God for direction, we gain faith in his promises. When we are clearly in over our heads, God's loving hands will hold us up. We know that he is always near.

God fights for us.

Crossing Hurdles

At last the Spirit is poured out on us from heaven. Then the wilderness will become a fertile field . . . [that] will yield bountiful crops.
Isaiah 32:15

If you've ever driven coast-to-coast across the States, you know the varied terrain of our great country. The midsection often seems like a vast wilderness, but I owe my heritage to the Great Plains, and I return eagerly, enjoying the rugged beauty of the region.

Crossing the wilderness of life is tough, but it's often the only way to reach our dreams. The Israelites had to live in the wilderness before they could enter the Promised Land. The wilderness in our own lives also teaches faith, patience, perseverance, dedication, and the strength of God's guidance and power.

The dreams God gives us pull us out of our comfort zones and move us toward our true selves. We must often cross a wilderness on the way to fulfillment. The desert confirms our goals, forges our faith, and strengthens our will.

Begin living in pursuit of your God-given dreams, and move closer to God. The hurdles to be crossed will require your courage and perseverance.

Step out in faith toward your God-honoring dreams today!

Honor your God-given dreams.

Leaving Footprints

They share freely and give generously to those in need.
Their good deeds will be remembered forever. They will
have influence and honor. Psalm 112:9

One of the great pleasures in life is spending a day walking barefoot through the sand and surf at a beach. The soft sand combines with the rhythmic lapping of the sea to create a mysterious beauty. We leave a trail of footprints, and as they are gently erased by the swirling sea, we are reminded of our brief humanity.

How and where we walk affects the world around us. God hopes that our lives will leave the imprint of our character, like footprints in the sand.

How can we leave a legacy with our lives? Consider where your heart is drawn. Donate your time and energy generously to people and causes that you feel passionate about. It might be a literacy class or a teenage pregnancy program. Many lives are in need of help and a little guidance. Find a way to leave a footprint by investing in the lives of others through giving of your own experience. Though our lives are busy, paring down our nonessential activities frees time for legacy leaving.

Leave the world a better place than you found it!

Leave a legacy!

Computer Crash

I prayed to the LORD, and he answered me. He freed me from all my fears. Those who look to him for help will be radiant with joy.
Psalm 34:4-5

A writer's computer is a very important tool. Yesterday, I learned its extreme importance when my computer crashed. Yes, this beloved instrument I am writing on today caused unprecedented chaos yesterday. After hours spent in restoring and reloading files, I thanked God that I had the foresight to create external backups.

As problems arise, our worlds seem to tumble down, but God regards our problems as his opportunities. Through facing our problems, we learn many valuable lessons.

In conquering our difficulties with God's help, we gain wisdom, respect his power, and choose to obey him. Coming through troubled times gives us greater confidence and turns our fear into faith; we know firsthand where our help comes from.

Don't let tribulations generate discouragement and despair. Stay in step with God, trust his leading, and give every situation your best effort! God wants to turn your problems into pathways of promise, and bring his love into your life in astonishing ways.

God is with us in difficult times.

Ripe Harvest

The fields are already ripe for harvest. The harvesters are paid good wages, and the fruit they harvest is people brought to eternal life. What joy awaits both the planter and the harvester alike! John 4:35-36

Autumn conjures quiet memories of wool plaid jackets, the warmth of bonfires, scratchy straw on a horse-drawn hay wagon, crisp days, and chilly nights. As the yellow harvest moon dominates the evening sky, we enjoy apples, pies and hot cider, friendship and laughter. Autumn is a time for harvest and celebration.

Jesus talked to his disciples about a harvest of people who were ready to give their lives to Jesus. A harvester enters his fields to gather fruit and grain for the table. Jesus' harvest brings willing hearts to God as we share the hope we have with those around us. What better celebration is there in life than the joy of bringing a precious life to the Lord! We live knowing that we will have eternal life with Christ, and this spreads hope to a hurting world.

Enjoy the season's cider, hayrides, and pumpkins. Enjoy a harvest of love and shared hope. Catch the spirit of the season and celebrate!

Jesus gives us hope!

The Masquerade

When the cool evening breezes were blowing, the man and his wife heard the Lord God walking about in the garden. So they hid from the Lord God among the trees.

Genesis 3:8

Life can seem like a costume party. In the masquerade of daily living, we strain to measure up by hiding behind our masks. However, struggling to be someone we are not hides the beauty of our true selves. Putting aside pretense brings truth and life.

The masquerade began with God's first human creatures, Adam and Eve. After Eve had tasted the forbidden fruit and shared it with Adam, they knew their fault and saw how far they had fallen. They knew that they did not measure up, so they hid to cover their shame. Centuries later, we continue the same masquerade.

When we come out of hiding, we leave our shame behind and enter the light of God's love. God accepts and loves us just as we are, and he remembers that he formed us from dust. We don't need to meet impossible standards, but we need to be our true selves.

Jesus came to forgive our imperfections and restore us to God. Come into his light and experience the joy of being real!

Come out of hiding.

Flight Communication

The earnest prayer of a righteous person has great power and produces wonderful results. James 5:16

Flying the friendly skies is a big job these days. The safety of the passengers who travel worldwide, and the people on the ground, depend on the pilots' effectiveness. Pilots may be top-notch in training and skills, but without communication, they cannot fly safely. A plane may know its own location, but it has no way to manage the weather, avoid other airplanes, or touch down onto the proper runway without proper communication with its flight control tower.

Flying the friendly skies of life is also a big job. Our attitudes affect the lives of those around us. We may be first-class people, but without constant communication with God, our lives are ineffective. Communication with God is essential to staying on course. Prayer is our most powerful resource.

Prayer is not bargaining with God to get our own way or controlling God to gain personal success. True prayer is constant communication with a personal, omnipotent God who aligns our life's course with his. When we pray, we tap into God's power, and our lives become effective.

God guides our lives.

Eternal Things

Anyone who believes in God's Son has eternal life.

John 3:36

Today, our lives easily become wrapped up in productivity, profit margins, stock prices, and pay scales. Every economic factor has its glory days and not-so-glorious days. It is hard to base our lives or our jobs on the performance of a fleeting economy. We are told in the Bible of a love that never changes and never ends. This is a love we can bank our lives on.

The New Testament repeatedly speaks of God's incredible offer of eternal life. If eternal life is really our destiny, why do we spend so much of our time caught up in things that won't matter past today? We are driven toward acquiring more—having more money, power, and possessions. While we're good at being productive, we often feel empty on the inside.

God has more in mind for our lives than lonely crowds and empty hearts. God wants us to begin living from an eternal perspective, thinking of things that have value in heaven: building relationships, using our God-given talents, and making a mark on the world for him. Don't fill your days with meaningless activity; live in the light of God's love. It will guide you to the things that matter most.

Focus on heavenly things.

Wings of the Wind

O LORD my God, how great you are! You are robed with honor and majesty. You are dressed in a robe of light. You stretch out the starry curtain of the heavens. . . . You make the clouds your chariot; you ride upon the wings of the wind. Psalm 104:1-3

God created nature with outstanding color and graceful forms. There are dramatic natural scenes, and the quiet beauty of flowers, birds, and butterflies. Our most lavishly sequined gown could never compare with a dew-glistening rose petal at sunrise. God cares for nature's every need. No human song could outperform the goldfinches' sweet music. It reminds us to trust God with our talents and let our lives unfold as he would wish.

As humans, we have a deep longing to connect with God, and we need to experience him on a natural level. Our original purpose, given by God at Creation, was to care for the earth and its creatures.

One great way to fulfill this purpose is to intentionally connect with nature. Plan a trip to the mountains, plains, or ocean, and experience God's greatness. Take a walk to enjoy the sunrise, and use the fresh air to rejuvenate your spirit. Find joy in nature today!

Nature pleases and renews us.

Acceptance—No Exceptions

Zacchaeus quickly climbed down and took Jesus to his house in great excitement and joy. But the people were displeased. "He has gone to be the guest of a notorious sinner," they grumbled.   Luke 19:6-7

Jesus encountered disapproving attitudes in the churchy people of his day. When he spoke to a man named Zacchaeus, the crowds were openly displeased. "Jesus responded, 'Salvation has come to this home today. . . . For the Son of Man came to seek and save those who are lost'" (Luke 19:9-10). Zacchaeus was a despised, cheating tax collector, but Jesus loved him. In response, Zacchaeus changed his ways and followed Jesus.

Each day, we have opportunities to accept the people who enter our lives, as Jesus did. Regardless of background or social status, Jesus sees each person as a precious life in need of a Savior. When we see through his eyes, we realize that each human life is precious and worthwhile.

Look for ways to include the people with whom you interact. Invite them to coffee, to church, or to your home. As we open our lives to being used by God, the world will be changed, one heart at a time.

Break down the walls of exclusion and love as Jesus does.

Jesus accepts sinners like us!

Empowering Words

Those who control their tongue will have a long life;
opening your mouth can ruin everything.   Proverbs 13:3

All of us have vivid memories of hurtful words. Whether
they are from siblings, parents, bosses, or peers, harsh
words pierce the soul. One of our bodies' smallest muscles
often exerts the most influence. Words can build others up
or cut them to the core. Our words need to be used with
care.

James 3 is primarily concerned with our power of speech.
"If we could control our tongues, we would be perfect and
could also control ourselves in every other way" (James 3:2).

Our mouths reveal what is in our hearts. Instead of
jealousy, uncontrolled anger, selfishness, and condescen-
sion, the Holy Spirit helps us to express love, joy, peace,
patience, kindness, goodness, faithfulness, gentleness and
self-control (see Galatians 5:22-23).

Enrich your relationship with Jesus, the only source
of life-giving words. Talk to him about your patterns of
speech. Ask him to help you control hurtful words of
manipulation, gossip, complaints, and lies. Rely on God
to help you speak empowering, encouraging, life-building
words.

Our tongues wield great influence.

In Laughter and Sorrow

There are "friends" who destroy each other, but a real friend sticks closer than a brother. Proverbs 18:24

I remember well the last time I laughed so hard that I cried. Such memories—times when our bellies hurt and our mascara runs down our cheeks—are the very essence of life. Share a great laugh with friends and loved ones; life is too short to be lived without laughter. But life isn't always about laughing; sometimes we need to cry with someone instead. Life is made for sharing intimately with others, in laughter and in sorrow. As Jesus walked the earth, he made relationships with God and with others his top priority.

Having great friends and family requires much of us. Real friendships don't happen overnight. We must take an active role in every great friendship—giving devotion to people and not just achievements, choosing connections with others over selfish ambition, and investing time in building others up and not just in building our bank accounts. In the significant achievement of deep friendship, we experience a meaningful, joyful life.

Having friends to laugh, cry, and grow old with is one of life's greatest experiences.

Enjoy the blessings of friendship!

Eye for Beauty

God has made everything beautiful for its own time. He has planted eternity in the human heart, but even so, people cannot see the whole scope of God's work from beginning to end.   Ecclesiastes 3:11

Just as God knows the number of apple seeds in one apple, God knows the full potential of our lives. Our view of life is limited, for we have trouble seeing as God sees. Each of our lives is a thread in the fabric of God's master plan.

As a sculptor sees the masterpiece in the stone before beginning to work, God sees the end in the beginning of things. He works carefully, unveiling our beauty day by day, stroke by stroke with his divine chisel. As we submit our lives to the Master's hands, we become more like the masterpiece he has in mind.

Our lives are often frightening, and as the events of our lives leave us feeling helpless, we naturally pull inward and away from the Master Sculptor. If we realize that everything around us is a work in progress, we may be able to release our fears, trust God, and open our hearts to the gentle unveiling of our beauty.

We are beautiful in God's eyes.

Feeding the Birds

Ask the birds of the sky, and they will tell you. Speak to the earth, and it will instruct you. . . . For the life of every living thing is in his hand, and the breath of every human being. Job 12:7-10

As October draws to a close, daylight dwindles, grass withers, and the flowers are nearly spent. In the bleaker days of the year, we enjoy bringing nature close to home with a few bird feeders.

Years ago, we put out one goldfinch feeder. Now we hang feeders for other favorite birds, such as a suet feeder for colorful woodpeckers and a black-oil-sunflower feeder for cardinals and chickadees. Birds bring the fall and winter landscape to life, and our whole family enjoys the entertainment of opening our backyard to birds.

Job sheds some light on our need to connect with the natural world. He said that in observing and listening to nature, we discover that every living thing is held in God's hands.

Our lives are greatly enriched by connecting with nature. Slowing down enough to marvel at the rich colors of the songbirds and becoming involved in their care brings a deeper joy to life. Invite nature to your doorstep this season!

Feed the birds this winter.

Preparing for Christmas

Then the King will say to those on his right, "Come, you who are blessed by my Father, inherit the Kingdom prepared for you from the creation of the world."

Matthew 25:34

Every year, Christmas seems to come earlier. We are often unprepared. With a little foresight and planning, Jesus' birth can be a significant celebration without the stressfulness.

In our house, pageants and parties pick up as Christmas draws near. Unless I make deliberate preparations, I will be blinded by extra stress and miss all the fun. Thanksgiving, the traditional shopper's gift-buying time, is at different times each year, so I begin my Christmas planning at Halloween to have an eight-week lead.

Our Creator is orderly. He created a complex universe, and Jesus said that before Creation, God had already prepared his heavenly Kingdom for our arrival. If God planned ahead for our arrival, we would do well to begin our preparations for celebrating Jesus' arrival at Christmas.

Think about what you value at Christmas, and write these things down. Tomorrow, we will look at more ways to minimize the stress of the upcoming holidays so you can concentrate on Jesus in this special season.

Plan to celebrate Christ's birth.

Creating a Christmas Calendar

Look! I am sending my messenger, and he will prepare the way before me. Malachi 3:1

Consider the possibility of being organized for Christmas before the holiday rush this year! You can overcome the frustrations and omissions of years past. The family photograph and Christmas cards will be mailed on time and presents will be bought and wrapped before Christmas Eve. There will be less stress and more time to reflect on the meaning of Christmas.

When Jesus came to earth, God prepared the way for him. The entire Old Testament builds up to the birth of our Savior. Jesus' cousin, John the Baptist, prepared the way for Jesus' ministry.

Christmas celebrations can be organized from year to year with a notebook. Use it to record important events, vacation days, and celebrations. Next, fill in days for Christmas card writing and mailing, baking, and cleaning. Create a list of names and gifts, and begin shopping. When gifts are purchased, wrap and label them, and put them in a designated place. Accumulate helpful pages for decorating ideas, menus, and holiday attire. Then put on your favorite Christmas music, savor family traditions, and enjoy the special season of Christ's birth.

Minimize stressfulness this Christmas.

Living with Expression

Don't just pretend to love others. Really love them. Hate what is wrong. Hold tightly to what is good. Romans 12:9

I enjoy watching people in public places. I have noticed a stark contrast between children under ten and those who are older. When children see something really thrilling, such as brightly colored balloons, they do not hide their emotions. Their hearts are pure, and their faces reveal sheer delight or utter disappointment.

As adults, we learn to hide our feelings and keep quiet about them. Experience teaches us that expressing ourselves will set us up for disappointment, so we hide our true selves.

Perhaps God allows obstacles in our adult lives to wake us up to life. God wants us to fully experience the blessings and relationships that he places in our lives, and children can help us understand how to do this. God loves it when we acknowledge the life and love he gives us.

To experience these blessings, we need to remove the disguises of our hearts and open ourselves to the beauty and love around us. Enjoy the colors of autumn and the warm hugs of loving relationships. Experience God's joy today!

Live with an open heart.

Wings like Eagles

Those who trust in the LORD will find new strength. They will soar high on wings like eagles.   Isaiah 40:31

A soaring eagle is a vision of magnificent beauty. Wings outstretched, head held high against the azure sky, the majestic eagle rises in strength. We, too, can soar on wings like eagles, overcome life's obstacles, and rise above life's troubles.

God says that when we trust in him, we will soar. When we put our hope in him, we rest in a power greater than our own. An eagle flies high by riding a rising air thermal. We must tap into God's mighty power.

Instead of being tied down by things that don't go our way, we can offer them to our loving, all-capable God. He frees us from the cords that bind us, cares for our souls, and enables us to fly high. When we turn our difficulties over to God, leave them in his hands, and rest in patience and hope, God will give us his resources.

God is in control of our lives, and he has our best in mind. Release your troubles to God, rise up, and soar today.

Trust God and fly high.

The Gerbil Wheel

God has not given us a spirit of fear and timidity, but of power, love, and self-discipline.　　　2 Timothy 1:7

Not long ago, friends offered us three hand-me-down gerbils. What three boys would pass up three gerbils? As we watch these funny rodents, I marvel at how they enjoy running round and round on their wheel. They take pleasure and comfort in going nowhere!

Humans can also become complacent in their routines in much the same way that our gerbils are comfortable in their little cage. God does not want us to live in fear of venturing out of our comfort zones, but he hopes that we will trust in him and live courageously.

Fear of the unknown and of what others may say or do keeps us trapped in our little lives. When we're brave enough to think, pray, and trust beyond ourselves, we discover that a whole world of adventure is waiting for us.

Take a risk today! Explore your abilities and try out your creativity and talent. Try something new! Take those long-delayed music lessons, a photography course, or a cooking class. Travel to a new country, hike a local trail, or venture down a new road.

Allow God to create peace and joy, delight and bravery in you today.

Make some discoveries!

Fragrance of Our Lives

Our lives are a Christ-like fragrance rising up to God.
2 Corinthians 2:15

We look forward to family celebrations and holiday gatherings. We love the aroma and warmth of holiday breads, cookies, and pies. Many herbs and spices also liven up the season. They beckon guests to come on in and enjoy the comforts of food, friends, and festivities.

Paul writes that our lives have a beautiful fragrance. God enjoys the wonderful aroma of our love and joyful service, and our prayers rise up to him like incense. Imagine that! God loves the fragrance of our lives, and we give *him* joy!

This holiday season, create a beautiful fragrance with your life. Embrace the celebrations of the season and welcome people into your home. Give some thought to your environment, and enjoy your favorite seasonal fragrances of pumpkin, evergreen, or cinnamon.

Embrace your friends and family with warm hugs and warm attitudes, even if they are hard to love; in so doing, we become more like Christ. The beautiful fragrance of our lives will bring joy to our loving God and to those around us.

The fragrance of our lives pleases God.

Great Invitation

*The Kingdom of Heaven can be illustrated by the story
of a king who prepared a great wedding feast for his
son. When the banquet was ready, he sent his servants
to notify those who were invited. But they all refused to
come!*   Matthew 22:2-3

Our oldest son came bounding off the bus one day,
beaming with excitement. He and the rest of his class
had been invited to a classmate's birthday party at a new
WonderPark. When party time came around, however,
only a handful of kids showed up.

Jesus tells a similar story to illustrate humans' rejection
of his open offer of love and acceptance. Jesus came to earth
to pay the entire penalty for our sins. He died, conquered
death, and triumphantly rose again. Jesus invites us to eternal life with him—we simply need to accept it. In Jesus'
illustration, the invited guests all refused to come.

The invitation to live forever with God in heaven is
incredible! There is no greater choice in our lives than the
one to follow Jesus. We make a great decision if we choose
to accept his invitation. Jesus welcomes us with open arms!

We are invited to new life in Christ!

River of Life

Instead, I want to see a mighty flood of justice, an endless river of righteous living.
Amos 5:24

This autumn, the leaves are falling, and the streams are flowing purely and coolly with melting early snow. Our minds are transfixed as we gaze at the majestic creation surrounding us. There is something mesmerizing and mysterious about watching water rush and fall over smooth river stones. Perhaps sounds of water awaken our thirst for the One who brings truth and new life.

Sometimes, in our normal humanity, we just go through the motions. In our busy routines, we lose the perspective of a right relationship with God, who wants nothing more than our sincere hearts, full of love for him. We become like a dry riverbed without him, for he is the only source of life, worship, love, joy, and praise. As we seek God and turn our hearts and lives back to him, they are restored to us.

Jesus offers us living water from a source that will never run dry. When we connect with him in sincere thanksgiving and praise, our worship comes alive. We offer up life as cool and refreshing as a beautiful autumn river. Take time to seek him!

Jesus is the source of life!

Unanswered Prayers

He prayed that, if it were possible, the awful hour awaiting him might pass him by. "Abba, Father," he cried out, "everything is possible for you. Please take this cup of suffering away from me. Yet I want your will to be done, not mine."
Mark 14:35-36

In life, it is natural to have many hopes and dreams. We pray that certain things will happen, yet inexplicably, they do not. We wait for healing, for better relationships, for a spouse, for a baby. We may not understand the answers to our prayers, but we have the joy of knowing that God is in control.

Jesus prayed agonizingly in the garden of Gethsemane before his crucifixion. He hoped and prayed that God would take away his coming suffering, but he knew that God's will was more important than his own comfort. Without Jesus' death on the cross and his triumph over death, we would not have God's perfect gift of eternal life. God knows best, and sometimes prayers are better left unanswered.

God wants to fulfill our dreams and answer our prayers, but our prayers don't always fit his plan. Unanswered prayer is a blessing, for God's plans are always grander than we can imagine.

God's joy is worth waiting for.

Clear Directions

What does the Lord your God require of you? He requires only that you fear the Lord your God, and live in a way that pleases him, and love him and serve him with all your heart and soul.　　　Deuteronomy 10:12

The Bible is a thick and sometimes intimidating book. Its stories are about healing, love, truth, and trust. Yet understanding even a little of what the Bible says and applying it to daily lives can be difficult.

Sometimes we wonder, *What am I here for? What does God expect of me? How do I know when I'm doing the right things?* Deuteronomy answers that God desires our respect, right living, sincere love, wholehearted service, and direct obedience. Jesus said, "You must love the Lord your God with all your heart, all your soul, and all your mind . . . [and] love your neighbor as yourself" (Matthew 22:37-39).

God does not appreciate complicated religious rules and requirements. He wants to give us eternal life, have a rich daily friendship with us, and fill our lives with his joy. Living for Jesus brings deep satisfaction and peace here on earth.

God wants us to live in love.

Liven Up the Living Room

Since I live, you also will live.   John 14:19

Most modern homes have a living room. The title is rather funny because it is usually the least lived-in room in the house. It gets passed up for our society's new kind of living . . . watching television. With hundreds of channels at our fingertips, it is easy to plop down in front of the screen and while the hours away. Soon, the day ends, without much interaction or activity.

Jesus had much to say about living. He wanted us to enjoy a life of greater quality, hope, joy, and love. He gave his life so that we could receive eternal life.

Wouldn't it be great to have more vitality in our daily lives? Instead of blankly watching a screen, we could share conversation, relax with music, and enjoy good books and food. Why not bring more life to the living room?

Give yourself permission to rethink this neglected space. Invest in some comfy, oversized chairs. Place good lamps, bookshelves, and media baskets nearby. Add some music and invite your loved ones to sit down for a while.

A room for relaxing with the simple joys of conversation and reading will bring peace and life into your home.

Enjoy a simpler life.

Crumbles at a Touch

Anyone who listens to my teaching and follows it is wise, like a person who builds a house on solid rock.

Matthew 7:24

In autumn, I love to find a birdhouse or two to add interest to the winter landscape. Sometimes I find a cheap but beautiful birdhouse. After the snows, thaws, rain, and ice, cheap birdhouses crumble at a touch. The costlier cedar birdhouses last longer.

As humans, we sometimes choose the path of least resistance. In our house, we call that being "penny smart, dollar dumb." We'll do anything to save a penny, but in the long run, we pay much more for having chosen the easier, cheaper route.

Jesus illustrates this concept with a story about two men building houses. One built his home on the rock along the shore. It cost him a lot of time, money, and effort, but when the storms of life came along, his house stood strong. The other man built his house penny smart on the sand, and of course, his house was washed away.

The shiny things of life tempt us to take shortcuts, but they usually wash away in life's storms. If we build our lives day by day on God's Word, our lives will withstand any test.

Build your life on the Rock.

Warm Welcomes

The Word gave life to everything that was created, and his life brought light to everyone. The light shines in the darkness, and the darkness can never extinguish it.

John 1:4-5

As the natural light dims with the approach of winter, we have to turn on the house lights more often. Their warmth shines through our windows to welcome others. Our neighbors, friends, and peers are in our lives for a reason. Welcome them into your life and home. Hang a wreath to warm up your home's front door.

The first few verses of John's Gospel describe Jesus as God's light. John calls Jesus "the Word" as he speaks of the unprecedented life and light he brought into the world. Jesus is the answer to all of our questions and the remedy for our ailing hearts.

Our eyes are the windows of our bodies. Most of us can tell when something is wrong by looking in the eyes of our family members and friends. When our lives shine with Christ's love, our eyes also shine. Allow Christ's love and light to shine through your life into the lives of others. He will light your path through the darkness. Shine for him today!

Jesus' light outshines any darkness.

Normal, Extraordinary Days

This is the day the LORD has made. We will rejoice and be glad in it.
Psalm 118:24

The sun rises and sets, and with family, work, and other commitments, our days are filled to overflowing. In our fast-paced world, the interruptions of phone calls, e-mails, and children occur at least once every ten minutes.

Since our lives are busy and time goes fast, we need to spend a few minutes each day listening in order to be aware of what we really want to do. Make plans to do these things. Today is a precious gift from God; it should be used for what really matters!

Though it is hard to make time to do something special, those special things need to be done. Today may be the only opportunity to break out of your familiar routine to do something extra.

Plan dinner with friends, have a pizza picnic with the kids, celebrate with a loved one, send a handwritten note, take photographs, and invest time in nurturing yourself. These important things can be done with a little extra effort and energy.

Make a precious gift of today. Make lasting memories out of little things. That's what an extraordinary life is made of!

Make today extraordinary!

Art of Creation

In the beginning God created the heavens and the earth. The earth was formless and empty, and darkness covered the deep waters. And the Spirit of God was hovering over the surface of the waters. Then God said, "Let there be light," and there was light. Genesis 1:1-3

Before time began, in darkness and emptiness, God imagined amazing colors. In blazing yellow, God set forth the light. Then colors of every hue on the spectrum appeared, all from God's creativity. The fair green of meadows and the deep green of forests; the dark blue of vast waters and the clear turquoise off sandy beaches; the blazing orange of autumn foliage and the delicate orange of monarch wings; the blooming purple of wildflower meadows and the majestic purple-hued mountain peaks; warm, earthen deserts and gray frozen tundra were all created by the Artist. God imagined and created, and he said, "It is good."

Since we are made in the creative image of God, we can appreciate his artistry by enjoying nature and by using our own imagination and creativity. When we create, we become more like God. Our artistry makes an impact on the world by bringing color and variety out of monotony. In creating, we find joy.

We were made to create.

Powerful Position

When Simon Peter realized what had happened, he fell to his knees before Jesus and said, "Oh, Lord, please leave me—I'm too much of a sinner to be around you."

Luke 5:8

One day along the beach, Jesus met a few fishermen. They had worked all night without catching a single fish, and they were exhausted and frustrated. When Jesus asked them to cast their nets just one more time, the fishermen caught more than their nets could hold. Both boats nearly sank from that catch. Simon Peter fell humbly to his knees, recognizing his unworthiness before Jesus' greatness.

Jesus comes into our lives to offer us fulfilled dreams and barely imagined hopes. When we obey his directions by going out in our boats just one more time, our nets are filled with his blessings.

So often, we work hard for hours on end with no progress. When we reach too high for things, we forget whose power makes the greatest and most amazing things happen. If we're going to reach for anything in life, we need to get on our knees. When we are humble and draw on Jesus' power, all things are possible.

Get on your knees to reach great heights.

Potential and Promise

So encourage each other and build each other up, just as you are already doing. 1 Thessalonians 5:11

God visibly works in miracles. He starts a raging fire with a single spark, a hurricane with a single raindrop, new lives with a single cell, and beautiful flowers with a single seed. God creates each human life with enormous potential and promise. The world may not see it, but God does.

God knows our hearts. He sees in a child the woman she is becoming, despite her childish behavior. God sees our brave hearts in the midst of fear. He sees the little grain of faith that can grow into a great work for him. He knows the impact of a single willing heart on the world, and the beauty that evolves from our imaginations. God encourages us to be all that we were meant to be.

We need the encouragement of daily time with God, or our hearts will be driven by selfish desires. Pray for God's plan to be revealed step-by-step in your life. Orient your heart toward him. In gratitude, allow your life to encourage others along God's path as well.

Encouragement transforms our lives.

Speed Bumps

No one will be able to stand against you as long as you live. For I will be with you as I was with Moses. I will not fail you or abandon you. Be strong and courageous.

Joshua 1:5-6

Even when speed bumps are painted bright yellow, they sometimes catch me off guard. In the fast lane of life, speed bumps often appear without warning. After hitting the rough patch of a job loss, the death of a loved one, a cross-country move, or a broken relationship, we struggle to keep rolling along. Speed bumps are hard on us.

Our Lord promises to be with us through the bumps, but not to take the hardships away. If we had no challenging mountains to climb, we would not grow stronger. God allows the battles of our lives to bring growth, to demonstrate his work in our lives, and to draw us closer to him.

God promises to direct and provide for our life's journey. When we trust him and follow his leading, we will have direction and stability. He will be near us and comfort us.

God longs to bless us with his presence. Trust in his promises, and he will lead. Believe, and all things will be possible.

God is with us.

Anchors for Life

This hope is a strong and trustworthy anchor for our souls.
Hebrews 6:19

We often feel unsure and fearful in this constantly changing world. God's promises reassure us. This short list of promises from the Bible can anchor your life to his love.

God is unchanging: "I am the LORD, and I do not change." (Malachi 3:6)

God gives us direction: "I will lead blind Israel down a new path." (Isaiah 42:16)

God is always with us: "Don't be afraid, for I am with you." (Isaiah 41:10)

God is our strength: "I will strengthen you and help you." (Isaiah 41:10)

God protects us: "He will order his angels to protect you." (Psalm 91:11)

God always forgives: "He has removed our sins." (Psalm 103:12)

God is our salvation: "Believe in the name of the Son of God so that you may know you have eternal life." (1 John 5:13)

God is our friend: "I know you by name." (Exodus 33:17)

God's promises anchor our lives.

Held in Balance

Our lives are in his hands, and he keeps our feet from stumbling.

Psalm 66:9

In our active house, with three constantly running young boys, pictures often come off the walls. They are not taken down gently, but are inadvertently knocked off balance and crash to the hardwood floor. Brian is now expert at resetting cracked frames, and I am becoming accustomed to the broken-and-glued look—and the crashing sound.

Our lives are often like those poor pictures: We are easily knocked off balance. In life, things never seem to go smoothly. Just when we count on the expected, the unexpected comes along and knocks us off kilter.

Why do the smallest things upset our balance?

When our lives are strongly held in our loving Father's hands, we can rest assured that though the picture may be knocked off balance and sway to and fro on the wall, it will not fall. Our lives are held in place by hands of strength, love, and power. No matter what today brings, Jesus can handle it. We don't need to come unglued.

Today, rest in his hands and ask him to keep your life in balance.

God keeps us from falling.

Girls and Their Bags

*I have not achieved it, but I focus on this one thing:
Forgetting the past and looking forward to what lies
ahead.*   Philippians 3:13

Shuffling around in mommy's high heels, fancy hat, and shiny beads, with a little purse dangling from her shoulder, a young girl loves dressing up. A few years later, tiny teenage purses are used for car keys and a driver's license, evolving into bigger bags that will hold a growing number of accessories. As we grow, so do our purses. Purse accessories aren't the only things that accumulate as we grow up; another accessory of growing up is the baggage of guilt and worry. We take it along each day, and it weighs us down.

Paul writes in Philippians of a healthier, baggage-free way to live that pleases God and makes room for joy. He says that we need to forget the past and look to the future. Living in the present and looking forward to the future helps us to let go of burdens from the past. This frees us up for joy!

All of us need more joy, yet we all hold tightly to mistakes and regrets from yesterday. God wants us to clean out our bags to make room for joy!

Make room for joy!

The Riches of Joy

When troubles come your way, consider it an opportunity for great joy.
James 1:2

If having a joyful life depended on circumstances and things, our nation would be by far the most joyful. Although most of us believe that we don't have enough of what we need, our nation is very wealthy, with plenty of food to eat, clothes to wear, water to drink, and channels to watch. Most of the things we have are more than we really need.

Poverty-stricken countries have shortages of food and clean water, clothes, and electricity, yet people there some-times have riches of joy, love, and thankfulness that we tend to lack. Our country suffers from a far greater poverty of spirit.

James wrote of the problems that we inevitably face in life, saying that our reactions to life's troubles indicate the richness of our lives. When we are rich in joy, we can be thankful despite our problems instead of complaining when we experience suffering.

Imagine our transformation if we experienced joy even during hard times. Troubles do not have to steal our joy. Choose to learn and grow from the hard times. This will make you rich beyond belief!

Joy is the gift of choice!

Adorned with Jewels

*I am overwhelmed with joy in the L*ORD *my God! For he has dressed me with the clothing of salvation and draped me in a robe of righteousness. I am like a . . . bride with her jewels.*   Isaiah 61:10

When I was a little girl, I stayed up late to watch the legendary royal wedding of Princess Diana on television. What beauty she possessed in her bejeweled white gown, glittering crown and veil, and a train as long as forever! With her trademark grace and gentle beauty, Princess Diana was a very beautiful bride.

The Bible often speaks of God's people as his bride. Psalm 45:11 says, "For your royal husband delights in your beauty; honor him, for he is your lord." We rarely see ourselves as beautiful women whom God has created and loved, but God loves *you* and rejoices in your beauty. God hopes that you will live each day fully, and fulfill the purpose for which he created you.

God sees you as a beautiful bride adorned with jewels and dressed elegantly in white. When we open our hearts to his love for us, God clothes us in his love. Open your life to him today!

You are God's beautiful bride!

Moving toward Joy

When Jesus saw him and knew he had been ill for a long time, he asked him, "Would you like to get well?"

John 5:6

Jesus saw a man who had been lying near the pool of Bethesda in Jerusalem, waiting to be healed for thirty-eight years! Crowds of sick people waited near the pool, for they believed that if they were the first to touch the pool when the water stirred, they would be healed. This particular lame man could not move, so he missed every opportunity to touch the pool. Jesus asked him, "Would you like to get well?"

So often we suffer from one or more forms of unhealthiness. Like the lame man with his faith in the pool, we put our faith in doing things to make ourselves well. When we put our faith in Jesus and live in friendship with him, we discover healing . . . and joy.

Jesus asks if we would like to get well. Often, we feel more comfortable with the mess than with the freedom that health brings. It is hard to have the courage to move toward healing, but joy is always waiting beyond the mess.

Move toward healing and fuller life that Jesus offers.

Do you want to be healed?

Seeing Life's Miracles

Just as you cannot understand the path of the wind or the mystery of a tiny baby growing in its mother's womb, so you cannot understand the activity of God, who does all things.   Ecclesiastes 11:5

Imagine a tiny seed, floating and landing, grounding itself and waiting. Rain and sunlight swell the seed to bursting, and it puts down roots. Pairs of leaves pop out, catching more light. Slowly, the seed becomes a seedling and then a fledgling plant. As the days and nights pass and the earth warms, a bud forms and blooms, shining in its brief glory of vibrant colors and silken petals. From its fading beauty, a multitude of seeds form to fall and restart the cycle of life.

We will never fully understand life, but with each mystery, we catch a glimpse of the Master's hand. Each of us can see life as a beautiful series of miracles. In the difficult unknowns of life, we can choose to trust God and have deep joy, or we can allow things we don't understand to rob us of pleasure.

Choose joy; open your eyes and witness the miracles unfolding around you. Look for the places where God touches our world. Reach out and receive his love today!

God's miracles unfold around us!

Celebrate!

We were filled with laughter, and we sang for joy. And the other nations said, "What amazing things the Lord has done for them." Yes, the Lord has done amazing things for us! What joy!   Psalm 126:2-3

There is a spirit of celebration in all of life—the blaze of a fire, the bright colors of a bouquet, the comfort of hot chocolate with marshmallows, the time spent gazing at a beautiful sunset. We celebrate life because we have so many things to be thankful for. We celebrate by embracing each new day and by caring for ourselves and our loved ones. In the celebrations of life, each new day provides time to share, to love, and to grow.

Perhaps the root of joy—the greatest need of our lives—is an attitude of gratitude. When we are thankful for what we have been given, we are able to be filled with joy. When God brings us through something difficult, we can be thankful.

Live in gratitude for what you have been given. Being thankful for God's love will refresh your mind and heart and bring you joy. Begin with thankfulness and live joyfully today!

Thankfulness begets joy!

Candy-Counter Woes

Come, let us sing to the LORD! . . . Let us come to him with thanksgiving. Psalm 95:1-2

Who wouldn't love colorful packages with bright, shimmering labels promising sugary delights of every shape and flavor? Children encounter candy heaven with every trip through the checkout lane. As my boys drool over the splendid assortment of sweets, I wonder for the millionth time why retailers make it so hard on kids. It is hard for children to accept yet another candy denial and be thankful for the peanut butter sandwich waiting at home.

As grown women, we also have a hard time being content with what we already have. It's easy to whine and complain when we want new clothes or a coordinating faucet or another pair of shoes. Being thankful is especially hard when we are constantly shown more things that we could have.

God hopes that we will live in contentment and thankfulness instead of complaining about what we lack. When we are focused on God and the great things he does for us, we have no reason to grumble.

Place your eyes on God, our great Provider. He loves to hear our sincere thanks and praise.

Focus on your blessings.

From Coal into Diamonds

Be thankful in all circumstances, for this is God's will for you who belong to Christ Jesus.   1 Thessalonians 5:18

Life can be incredibly disappointing. We can always find a reason to grieve and complain. We often wait to live until life gets better . . . but often it does not.

Even if we suffer, wilt, and waver under the high pressures and hardships life brings us, we will not fall if we rely on our Lord for strength. He always has a glorious purpose just over the horizon, though not everything will go as we wish. God has his reasons for the suffering in our lives.

Coal, a normally undesirable form of the element carbon, is transformed under high pressure and temperature into diamonds, the most dazzling beauty known to humans. Just as black carbon becomes a priceless diamond, so our lives are transformed into something precious through the hardships we face. God strengthens us and gives us opportunities to grow and mature. God loves us and enables us to keep growing, using the hard times to create beauty out of pain.

We can be thankful for the tough times; life's pressures bring beauty to our lives.

Beauty can result from hardship.

Stacking Sandbags

Let us lift our hearts and hands to God in heaven.

Lamentations 3:41

When we lived in a hurricane-prone coastal region, we experienced many hurricane preparations and evacuations. Days before they hit land, hurricanes were known to be barreling toward the coast, gaining speed and strength. There was plenty of time to wait, worry, and want to do something, so many people began sandbagging. We worked very hard to prevent something that was out of our control from wrecking our lives. It felt good to *do* something about our concerns.

It is said that when we work, we work, and when we pray, God gets to work. I want God on my side, working for what is precious to me, but it is hard for me to turn my concerns over to him and to stop worrying. Our natural tendency is to build walls of worry and stack sandbags of anxiety instead of turning things over to God.

Prayer is our most important act regarding life's concerns. In prayer, we remember that our great God is bigger than any earthly problem.

Lift your heart up to God and exchange your worries for his peace.

Give your concerns to God.

Flower of Joy

Let your roots grow down into him, and let your lives be built on him. Then your faith will grow strong in the truth you were taught, and you will overflow with thankfulness.   Colossians 2:7

One year, one of our boys brought home a science experiment from school. His class had been studying plant growth and the teacher sent a sunflower seed home with each student. We were to plant it and watch it grow.

What a miracle bursts forth from a single seed! A lifeless pod of potential life, planted in soil, watered, and given light yields a new life! Atop the new sunflower plant is the gift of a sunny sunflower smile.

Our lives are also seeds. Without Jesus in our lives, we are dormant and lifeless. When we allow Jesus to fill our hearts, we come alive! What miracles burst forth from our lives! When we allow our roots to grow down deep into Jesus day by day while soaking up the sunlight of his Word, the flowers of our faith grow strong and beautiful.

Rooted in thanksgiving for all that Jesus has done for us, we find joy.

Joy grows out of thankfulness.

Saying Thank You

Give thanks for everything to God the Father in the name of our Lord Jesus Christ. Ephesians 5:20

Thank-you notes are fading in popularity amid the techno-communications of our lives. However, this personal touch of gratitude from one friend to another enriches our relationships. Handwritten thank-you notes take time, so when we receive one, we really appreciate it.

Our hurried society does not encourage gratitude. Popular culture seems to be thankful for nothing. It has a sense of entitlement about what it allegedly deserves, and assumes no debt of gratitude. If we've earned something, why should we say thank you?

Our great God, who faithfully sustains our every heartbeat, loves to be thanked. He knows that when we are thankful, we are not focused on ourselves, but on our undeserved blessings. In thankfulness, we recognize the sacrifice behind the gift.

In a culture where saying thanks is uncommon and the prevailing attitude is "I deserve it," you make a beautiful mark on your world when you say a sincere thank you. Take a few moments to sit down and write out your thoughts of gratitude to someone who has made a difference in your life. Make time to say thank you today!

Gratitude in life brings joy.

Find the Blessings

Praise God! Blessings on the one who comes in the name of the Lord!   John 12:13

A glass half full, or a glass half empty? It is less than a month until Christmas—with twenty-seven more opportunities to share the beauty and significance of the season. We can see the good side or the bad side of this, depending on how we look at it. We have expectations that don't turn out as we hope, but there is more to life than disappointment!

Studies have established that what we focus on will increase, and what we ignore will diminish. We can warm ourselves by being aware of a small source of heat, or let cold feet keep us awake.

There is beauty in each day and in each season. Choose to see beauty and allow yourself joy today. Look for reasons to be thankful. Regardless of the weather, we can choose to enjoy the day, because although we cannot control the weather, we can practice positive attitudes.

Put on your rain boots and take up your umbrella. With God at our side, we can enjoy stomping in the puddles. Even a rainy day is brighter when we choose an attitude of joy.

Today is the only day we have. Enjoy it!

Appreciate your blessings today!

Craziness of the Season

Indeed, the "right time" is now. Today is the day of salvation.   2 Corinthians 6:2

Three holiday parties next Saturday and no babysitter available, seven gifts to buy and wrap before the end of the week, forty-five Christmas cards to write, address, and mail—the Christmas to-do list seems overwhelming. What Christmas memories did you cherish as a child? Surely they were not about stress, long lines, or deadlines. The best memories are made of gingerbread cookies and warm pies, Christmas carols and frosty windows. They are not made of craziness.

Jesus came to give us rich, eternal life for now and for eternity. Start today by intentionally making room for the joys of the season. Today is the day to slow down and breathe.

Bring the overwhelming list into the light and cut it down to size. Say a guilt-free no to a few upcoming events in order to free up time to enjoy your family during this season. Make a list of more reasonable to-dos. Assign a time to work through your list in a leisurely way while enjoying Christmas music. Make this a Christmas season to remember; slow down and savor this time of welcoming our Savior into the world.

Invite Jesus for Christmas!

Heart-Filled Home

*If you want to enjoy life and see many happy days . . .
turn away from evil and do good. Search for peace, and
work to maintain it.*   1 Peter 3:10-11

The American dream is known worldwide—a house with a
two-car garage, a spouse, two kids, and a dog. Regardless of
our status according to that dream, we all long for a haven,
a place to rest our hearts.

Make a loving investment in your home. Don't hesitate
to line your shelves with treasures and create a comfortable spot to rest. Decorate for the Christmas season with
passed-along heirlooms, handmade crafts, much-loved
ornaments, and the familiar sounds of favorite Christmas
music. Make your home a place unlike any other—a place
that reflects you.

Though we all have different ideas on home and how to
enjoy it, one thing is certain. Once we have a place of peace
and joy, we must work hard to maintain it.

A home is a safe haven from the demands of life. Put
your heart into your home and find the treasures of joy and
peace.

Make Jesus the heart of your home.

Today's Joy

Always be full of joy in the Lord. I say it again—rejoice!
Philippians 4:4

Today is the day to take up living. Today is the day to enjoy the innocence of childhood with our children and grandchildren and experience family togetherness. Today is a great day to tell our loved ones how much we love them with a hug or flowers or a card. Our families and friends are God-given blessings. This is the time to enjoy them.

In a world filled with uncertainty and hardship, illness and wars, it is hard to imagine joy. Jesus said, "I have told you all this so that you may have peace in me. Here on earth you will have many trials and sorrows. But take heart, because I have overcome the world" (John 16:33).

Joy is different than happiness; it is based on the knowledge that our future is secure in Jesus. Despite our circumstances, we can be joyful knowing that Jesus has overcome the world.

Jesus wants us to thank him and tell him what we need. Our joy each day comes from Jesus' presence within us, and that can never be taken from us. Enjoy the wonderful times together. Whatever your circumstances, choose joy, because Jesus is on your side.

Jesus gives us joy!

Simply Live!

Therefore I . . . beg you to lead a life worthy of your calling, for you have been called by God. Always be humble and gentle. Be patient with each other, making allowance for each other's faults because of your love.
Ephesians 4:1-2

As we step out the back door into the snow, our breath fogs in the cold air. Thrilled by the first snowfall, we enjoy the simple beauty of the scene. Overnight, our brown world has been frosted with sparkling snow! What a pleasure to realize that God made all this for you and me!

God speaks to us through the beauty of creation. He calls us to become the people he created us to be before the beginning of time. As the silent beauty of the snowfall speaks volumes about God's love for us, our lives of humility and gentleness also communicate without words. God shines his life and joy through lives and hearts that are turned toward him.

Peter says, "If someone asks about your Christian hope, always be ready to explain it. But do this in a gentle and respectful way" (1 Peter 3:15-16). Live fully in God's love each day, and let his joy and gentleness speak through your life to the world around you.

God calls us to life!

Yesteryear's Ornaments

Sing a new song to the LORD! Let the whole earth sing to the LORD! Sing to the LORD; praise his name. Each day proclaim the good news that he saves.   Psalm 96:1-2

As we dig out our treasured ornaments to decorate the Christmas tree, many memories come flooding back. Some recall the joys of "Baby's 1st Christmas" or "Our 1st Christmas Together"; others bring a tinge of sadness. It is good to remember our past and look with clearer vision toward the future. In reflecting on our lives, we realize that life is short!

God knows that our lives are short. He hopes that we will make every day count and live each day fully. Life is too short for quarreling and manipulation, anger and selfishness. Each day is precious, and we should say "I love you" again and again.

Live as though each day were your last. We do not know what tomorrow holds; we only know that God's hands hold us each day. Don't worry about tomorrow or live in regret over yesterday. Be fully present to the opportunities God brings you today!

Thank God as you find joy in little things. Reconcile and forgive before the day is over. Enjoy making happy memories!

Live today without regrets!

Making the Impossible Possible

Your relative Elizabeth has become pregnant in her old age! People used to say she was barren, but she's now in her sixth month. For nothing is impossible with God.

Luke 1:36-37

From the very start, Jesus' life was a miracle. Every life begins as a miracle, but it was humanly impossible for Mary to be pregnant since she was a virgin. The angel Gabriel appeared to Mary and asked her permission for God to fill her with the Holy Spirit so that she could bear God's child! Impossible! Gabriel responded, "Nothing is impossible with God."

Mary was a poor, young, obedient Hebrew girl. Outwardly, Mary was an unlikely candidate to be used by God. However, the God who knows our names and the number of hairs on our heads also knows our hearts. God chose Mary to be the mother of his Son, Jesus. Mary accepted the mission and submitted to God's plan.

It is easy to doubt that our personal abilities amount to much. In God's eyes, all service to him begins with a willing and obedient heart!

Trust God, and allow him to make the impossible possible in your life!

Everything is possible with God!

The Fragrance of Christmas

She wrapped him snugly in strips of cloth and laid him in a manger.   Luke 2:7

Every perfume counter at the mall offers a new fragrance. Department stores are decked out in the sparkly splendor of the season. Beside every store's entrance, a person rings a bell and asks for donations. In a world decked out for the holidays, it is time to spend money on gifts wrapped in glittery papers. In the bustle of buying, we can be far from experiencing Christ's birth.

When Christ was born, he was not greeted by fragrant perfume, but by the aromas of a cow barn. Instead of the flashy lights we find in every store, Jesus was born under the pale light of a star. Instead of ringing bells and jingling money, Jesus heard the movements of cattle. There was no fanfare of radio jingles, but Jesus' birth was announced by the glorious radiance of an angels' choir. Jesus' world was far different from the world we know.

This Christmas season, step back from the familiar commercialism and experience the simple truth and beauty of Jesus' birth. Make time to reflect on the sights and smells, the sounds and feel, of Jesus' manger on that first Christmas Day. Jesus' gift of life began that starry night.

Imagine Jesus' Christmas.

Prince of Peace

For a child is born to us, a son is given to us. The government will rest on his shoulders. And he will be called: Wonderful Counselor, Mighty God, Everlasting Father, Prince of Peace.

Isaiah 9:6

Nearly seven hundred years before Jesus' birth, God gave the world a glimpse of the coming Messiah and a foretaste of his glory through the words of the prophet Isaiah. Wonderful, Mighty, Everlasting, and Prince of Peace are names that suggest the reality of our Holy God coming to earth in the flesh.

Jesus came to us through the wonder of a virgin birth. The wonder continued throughout Jesus' life and ministry as he performed miracles of healing and love for all people.

Jesus is the mighty God who defeated the power of death and sin when he gave his life for ours.

Because of Jesus' humble birth and selfless death on the cross, "instead of shame and dishonor, [we] will enjoy a double share of honor . . . and everlasting joy will be [ours]" (Isaiah 61:7).

In a bustling season known for extra stress, Jesus is our Prince of Peace.

Jesus was born to bring us his peace. Allow his everlasting joy to fill your life.

Jesus is our Prince of Peace!

Joyful Giving

Jesus . . . said, "I tell you the truth, this poor widow has given more than all the others who are making contributions. For they gave a tiny part of their surplus, but she, poor as she is, has given everything she had to live on."   Mark 12:43-44

As they put their last dimes together to heat their weathered homes, many families struggle to survive. A generous mom took a meal to one such family. As she prayed with them, she saw the extent of their need. Taking off her wool coat, hat, and shoes, she left them with the family, realizing that they needed them more than she did.

Each year, our country spends more for holiday gifts. Recently, holiday spending averaged over one thousand dollars per household. Giving to loved ones is a special way to celebrate Jesus' birth, but there are also many ways to celebrate by giving to those in need. For instance, one dollar per day cares for a child in poverty-stricken, AIDS-orphaned Africa. Children both around the world and next door need a helping hand to survive and to thrive.

Jesus encourages us to give to those in need with selfless joy. In giving, we fulfill Jesus' command to love.

Give to those in need.

The Beauty of Praise

Suddenly, the angel was joined by a vast host of others—the armies of heaven—praising God and saying, "Glory to God in highest heaven, and peace on earth to those with whom God is pleased."

Luke 2:13-14

Imagine being interrupted on a cold, dark night by an indescribably blinding light. From out of that radiance comes the voice of one—no, thousands upon thousands of voices lifted up in a heavenly chorus of praise. The shepherds on that first Christmas night must have shrunk back in fear at this sudden, bright symphony. Things like this did not happen every day out in the fields! The shepherds received personal notice of Jesus' wonderful birth. The awesome display prepared them to share the Good News and to rejoice and greet the newborn King. They were ready to meet Jesus!

In our darkened winter world, it is easy to be consumed with the bustle of Christmas and miss the awe of the season. For centuries, great music such as Handel's *Messiah* has been inspired by the angels' song recorded in Luke.

Churches, symphonies, radio stations, and musicals bring the Gloria to our busy world. Let the glorious sounds inspire you to meet Jesus at Christmas!

Enjoy the Gloria this Christmas!

Candy-Cane Christmas

So the Word became human and made his home among us. He was full of unfailing love and faithfulness. And we have seen his glory, the glory of the Father's one and only Son.   John 1:14

Years ago, a candy maker made a special candy to remind the world of Christ at Christmastime. He began with a pure white stick to symbolize the virgin birth and Jesus' sinless nature. He formed it into a *J* for Jesus, and turned it upside down to represent a shepherd's staff. He added three small red stripes and one large red stripe to represent Jesus' sacrifice on the cross. Of course, the candy became famously known as the candy cane.

   Jesus came to live among us. What incredible love God had for us, to send his only Son to live in human hardship and to die for our sins. We are undeserving of such love, yet God sends it lavishly into our lives!

   This Christmas, share the reason for your joy and hope with those around you. Make simple handmade gifts such as a candle circled by standing candy canes. Glue them on, tie them with a red ribbon, and attach the candy-cane story.

   Celebrate Christmas by lavishly spreading God's love to those around you!

Simple gifts express God's love.

To Reign in Our Lives

Mary responded, "Oh, how my soul praises the Lord. How my spirit rejoices in God my Savior! For he took notice of his lowly servant girl, and from now on all generations will call me blessed."
Luke 1:46-48

Imagine going about your daily life and having your personal hopes and dreams suddenly brought to a screeching halt. Some two thousand years ago, Mary's world was turned upside down in an instant. Perhaps she was daydreaming about her upcoming wedding to Joseph as she went about her chores when a surprise visitor stopped in without even opening the door. God sent the angel Gabriel to tell Mary that she would be pregnant with God's Son!

Mary was a virgin, engaged to be married. What would her parents, her society, and more importantly, her husband-to-be think of all this? Instead of falling apart, Mary answered, "I am the Lord's servant. May everything you have said about me come true" (Luke 1:38). Mary was open to serving the Lord with her whole being.

Every day, circumstances enter our lives that are beyond our control. We cannot know what God is planning for our future, but like Mary, we can open our hearts to God's call in our lives.

Respond faithfully to God's plans!

Open your heart to God!

Peaceful Holiday Relationships

You, O Bethlehem Ephrathah, are only a small village among all the people of Judah. Yet a ruler of Israel will come from you, one whose origins are from the distant past. . . . And he will be the source of peace. Micah 5:2, 5

What causes holiday stress for you? For some of us it is gathering gifts, mailing packages, or baking the traditional sweets, but for many of us, stress comes from gathering with relatives. No one has normal relatives. No one is perfect, and each of us gets on someone's nerves, especially when crammed into tight quarters with people we only see once a year! We must ask God for extra patience, love, and peace when we gather at Christmas!

Micah predicted Jesus' birthplace hundreds of years before he was born. Bethlehem means "the house of bread," which is fitting, since Jesus is the bread of life for a hungering world. Though Jesus was born in a humble stable in a small village, he came to be our source of life and peace. Only through him do we live fully or find peace that truly satisfies.

As you anticipate holiday gatherings with other less-than-perfect folks, remember that if you ask, Jesus will give you his peace and grace.

Enjoy peaceful Christmas gatherings.

Tree Topper

Where is the newborn king of the Jews? We saw his star as it rose, and we have come to worship him.

Matthew 2:2

Oh, the joy that a Christmas tree brings! I love to turn off the house lights and enjoy the beauty of our lighted Christmas tree in the silent house. Peace reaches out through the darkness and twinkles in the white lights.

Atop our Christmas tree sparkles a giant Christmas star that represents the star of the first Christmas. The Creator of billions of stars designed one special star to mark the place of his Son's birth. That star led the wise men to worship the infant Jesus.

The wise men saw this sign and passionately followed it for thousands of miles to worship the King who rested beneath it. May the stars that we see atop our trees also draw us to worship.

Let the star be a reminder of the meaning behind the hurry-scurry. May the star lead us to Jesus on Christmas even as we sit amid strewn wrapping paper. Jesus doesn't just want to be worshipped when we are standing in church. He wants us to bring him into the very heart of our lives.

Follow the star to Jesus!

Obviously Pregnant

At that time the Roman emperor, Augustus, decreed that a census should be taken. . . . Because Joseph was a descendant of King David, he had to go to Bethlehem in Judea, David's ancient home. . . . He took with him Mary, his fiancée, who was now obviously pregnant.

Luke 2:1, 4-5

No one can prepare a mother-to-be for nine months of an expanding waistline or for the trip to the hospital. With each child, our drive seemed longer. I can only imagine how the donkey ride felt to Mary!

Luke says that Mary was "obviously pregnant" when she traveled from Nazareth to Bethlehem. Any of us who have felt "obviously pregnant" know that Mary was uncomfortable. Donkey rides are rough at best, but Mary followed God's plans and traveled at just the right time.

The census issued by Augustus was one of a kind. God planned for Jesus to be born in Bethlehem, the City of David. Jesus arrived that starry night to just the right people, at just the right time and place.

Do you feel that you are in the wrong place in your life? Trust your life to God and allow him to guide you to the right place at the right time. Trust him today!

God accomplishes his plans.

Immanuel

Look! The virgin will conceive a child! She will give birth to a son, and they will call him Immanuel, which means "God is with us."   Matthew 1:23

What a difficult choice Joseph faced concerning his marriage to Mary! Joseph had two legal choices: divorce her or have her stoned to death. An angel of the Lord appeared to Joseph in a dream, saying, "Joseph, son of David, . . . do not be afraid to take Mary as your wife. For the child within her was conceived by the Holy Spirit" (Matthew 1:20). God presented a third option: Joseph could still take Mary as his wife. Joseph obeyed God and married Mary despite her pregnancy.

Life presents many difficult decisions and challenges. We make choices about how to use our time, money, and other resources. Many of our choices seem small, but each decision confirms our intention to please God or to please ourselves.

Our attitudes, tones of voice, and ways of relating may be our most important choices each day. Our decisions to follow God with our lives is part of each choice, large or small. With each decision, we need Joseph's integrity as we welcome Immanuel into our world. God is with us. May our lives manifest his presence!

Jesus is God with us.

Creatures of Habit

The angel said, "I am Gabriel! I stand in the very presence of God. It was he who sent me to bring you this good news! . . . Since you didn't believe what I said, you will be silent and unable to speak until the child is born." Luke 1:19-20

Our quirks define us. As small children, we begin building habits that last a lifetime. We have healthy lives when we build relational habits of loving acceptance, selfless forgiveness, and gentle patience. Habits of fly-off-the-handle anger and selfish manipulation tear relationships down. Responsible eating, exercise, and hygiene make for healthy bodies. Overeating and neglect are unhealthy habits.

According to Luke, our spiritual habits can also be healthy or unhealthy. The angel Gabriel appeared to Zechariah, the father of John the Baptist, to tell him that he and Elizabeth would have the baby they had long desired. Zechariah responded out of a habitual posture of doubt.

None of us are remotely perfect, but God hopes that we will grow in our spiritual lives each day to trust him and be more like him. Begin today to form healthy habits that will make you the woman God wants you to be!

Build good habits.

The Beauty of Being Ordinary

Elizabeth gave a glad cry and exclaimed to Mary, "God has blessed you above all women, and your child is blessed. . . . You are blessed because you believed that the Lord would do what he said."   Luke 1:42, 45

We're bombarded daily with media messages that proclaim the extravagant beauty of models and celebrities. Magazine covers and tabloid reports flaunt the characteristics of beauty that our world applauds. As consumers, we often validate the belief that youthfulness, thinness, curves, fashion, and wealth make us acceptable. When we step back and gain some perspective, we realize that artificial glamour does not hold a candle to the authentic beauty of God's Spirit in our lives.

Mary's relative Elizabeth was also told by an angel that she was carrying a special child. God blessed Mary and Elizabeth; they were ordinary women with extraordinary faith who were beautifully filled with God's radiance.

God asks each of us to serve him in unimaginable ways. God does not offer his gifts on the basis of our social status or fashionable beauty, but he teams up with those who have extraordinary faith.

Allow God to use you! God does great things through ordinary folks who offer him their hearts!

God gives ordinary people extraordinary faith!

Food and Friendship

A few days later Mary hurried to the hill country of Judea, to the town where Zechariah lived. She entered the house and greeted Elizabeth. At the sound of Mary's greeting, Elizabeth's child leaped within her, and Elizabeth was filled with the Holy Spirit.   Luke 1:39-41

Bright firelight and the glow of friendship bring warmth to these short winter days. However busy we become during this Christmas season, we still need to make time for friendship.

A few days after Mary heard the news of her pregnancy, she set off to visit her relative Elizabeth, who was pregnant with the baby who would be John the Baptist. Mary knew that time with a woman friend would help to smooth the rough places of her newly changed life. Elizabeth benefited as well; in Mary's presence, she was filled with the Holy Spirit. True friends multiply one another's joy.

Invite friends and loved ones for spontaneous hot cocoa by the fire or a friendly cookie swap. It doesn't matter if you share canned soup or drink tap water—the priceless value of female friends enriches the quality of our lives. Make time to get together with friends for support and laughter!

Share Christmas with friends and family.

Recognizing the Light

Simeon was there. He took the child in his arms and praised God, saying, "Sovereign Lord, now let your servant die in peace, as you have promised. I have seen your salvation, which you have prepared for all people. He is a light to reveal God to the nations!" Luke 2:28-32

A favorite Christmas tradition of ours is taking a drive to see the neighborhood lights. Some homes are simply decorated; others have big, bold lights and inflatable figurines in their yards. However we decorate for Christmas, the lights warm the air, illuminate the early nights, and lift our spirits.

A few days after Jesus' birth, Joseph and Mary took him to the Temple for the required ceremonies. There, a righteous elderly man named Simeon recognized the child. Simeon was so overjoyed to meet the Messiah that he scooped the baby Jesus up in his arms and praised God. Simeon called Jesus the "light to reveal God to the nations!"

Like the lights we use to celebrate his birth, Jesus came as the light of the world. Because of Jesus, we can see and know God. Because of Jesus, we can choose to believe— and live!

Build your life on the light that brings life—our Lord and Savior Jesus!

Jesus is our light!

Living in the Moment

*Mary kept all these things in her heart and thought
about them often.*   Luke 2:19

Sometimes we get so wrapped up in imagining a perfect
scenario that when the less than perfect comes along, the
opportunity and joy it offers are bypassed. At other times,
we are so caught up in what is not happening that we miss
out on what *is* taking place. If we're wrapped up in what
will happen tomorrow, or lamenting what happened yesterday, we miss the blessings of today!

   During the incredible events surrounding Jesus' birth,
Mary decided to live each moment fully. She kept the
events "in her heart and thought about them often." Part
of living in the moment is reliving important events until
we have fully grasped their significance.

   Mary wasn't too worried about how she looked or who
she could impress. Mary made the most of every moment.
She enjoyed the gift of the present each day. Even more
than two thousand years later, we have much to learn from
Mary.

   Let go of the loose ends in your life and give your
worries to God. Let today be a time to experience the joys
that come your way!

Savor each moment!

The Gifts We Bring

They entered the house and saw the child with his mother, Mary, and they bowed down and worshiped him. Then they opened their treasure chests and gave him gifts of gold, frankincense, and myrrh. Matthew 2:11

Three wise men from eastern lands followed the star of Bethlehem for thousands of miles to worship the newborn King. When they saw young Jesus, they bowed low in worship and offered him their treasures.

We sometimes bring gifts to God to try to prove our love. Through church volunteer hours, tithes, and religious rules, we give to the Lord out of a sense of duty.

The three wise men did not come to Jesus out of obligation, but out of sincere love. They were not there for what they could get, but to give him their adoration. Our greatest gift to Jesus is a heart filled with love and devotion. As Jesus said, "Wherever your treasure is, there the desires of your heart will also be" (Matthew 6:21). Jesus wants our hearts.

This Christmas, give Jesus the gift of your humble, joyful heart.

Jesus wants the gift of our hearts.

Seeing Him

They hurried to the village and found Mary and Joseph. And there was the baby, lying in the manger. After seeing him, the shepherds told everyone what had happened and what the angel had said to them about this child.   Luke 2:16-17

We live in a culture that values good impressions, so we try hard to be what we think other people expect. If others will accept us for being attractive, we try to achieve the slender, youthful image that our society adores. If acceptance is based on high intelligence, we earn academic credentials. If acceptance depends on what we do, we busy ourselves with worthy goals and accomplishments.

We see from the shepherds' story that God is not concerned with our accomplishments, intelligence, or looks. God sent the angels to humble shepherds in the sheep fields. In response to the joyful news, the shepherds did not try to make a good impression. They went as they were, and hurried to see the Savior!

God sees past our good impressions, and he wants us to see him for who he is.

Today, come as you are—and hurry to meet the newborn King!

Jesus accepts us as we are!

The Wonder of It All

The shepherds said to each other, "Let's go to Bethlehem! Let's see this thing that has happened, which the Lord has told us about."
Luke 2:15

"Jingle Bells," "Deck the Halls," and "Rudolph the Red-Nosed Reindeer" are stuck in our heads by this date, just two days before Christmas. Our Christmas card basket overflows with holiday greetings and annual updates from friends and loved ones. Our wallets are depleted, and a desk drawer is crammed with receipts and credit card statements.

Where is the feeling of Christmas? Where is the wonder that we long for at Christmastime? Where is the mention of Christ and his birth? We can go through the entire season and not even consider the purpose of the celebration!

Don't let the stress of travel, the overbooked holiday schedule, shopping, and wrapping cause you to miss out on the greatest piece of the holiday puzzle! We hear the Christmas story on Christmas Eve, but that doesn't mean that it actually registers. We sing "Hark, the Herald Angels Sing!" but we don't always celebrate the joyful news of the newborn Savior.

Take a pause and reflect on the wonder of it all.

Jesus is the source of all wonder.

Good News of Great Joy

I bring you good news that will bring great joy to all people. The Savior—yes, the Messiah, the Lord—has been born today in Bethlehem, the city of David!

Luke 2:10-11

Imagine if, as a small child, you opened every gift marked for you, and nothing was inside! You would be disappointed, sad, and perhaps angry—because your hope of finding something lovely inside the beautifully wrapped gift had been shattered.

We approach life hoping to find something spectacular inside. However, real life is hard; we are often disappointed when promises go unfulfilled. God's gift is that he will not leave us empty-handed; he did not design life to be an empty gift. When life gets hard, we find Jesus' hand holding ours, so we're never empty-handed!

The angels brought good news to the shepherds on that first Christmas night. When we approach each day with Jesus, we find joy because he fulfills all of our hopes! Instead of despair and loneliness, we find relationship. Instead of disappointment, we discover that our deepest longings are fulfilled. Discover his love and acceptance today!

God never leaves us empty-handed!

Lying in a Manger

You will recognize him by this sign: You will find a baby wrapped snugly in strips of cloth, lying in a manger.

Luke 2:12

The feelings of excited anticipation, the sound of scurrying padded footsteps, the sight of cascading stockings and long-awaited presents and a sparkling tree linger in all of our memories.

Imagine that first incredible Gift! Santa may bring things that we really *like,* but Jesus brings us the one thing we really *need*—the way to be saved from dying. Without him, we die a little more each day, but with Jesus in our lives, we can begin to really live!

That first Christmas morning, God sent his angels to give the greatest birth announcement ever to humble shepherds and their sheep. With all the glitz and sparkle of the holidays, we would expect Jesus to come first to the prestigious, the powerful, and the wealthy, but God reveals himself to plain and ordinary hearts that are humble enough to accept his gift. We find God's greatest gift "lying in a manger."

Jesus accepts us as we are, humble and open to life with Jesus. Accept God's incredible gift of life!

Jesus brings the gift of life!

Seeing Past Ourselves

*She never left the Temple but stayed there day and
night, worshiping God with fasting and prayer.* Luke 2:37

Herod the Great was king when Jesus was born. About the
time of Jesus' birth, "some wise men from eastern lands
arrived in Jerusalem, asking, 'Where is the newborn king
of the Jews? We saw his star as it rose, and we have come to
worship him'" (Matthew 2:1-2).

King Herod was greatly disturbed. Why? Because of his
pride! King Herod stewed and steamed and went something close to crazy before he decided how to handle this
newborn King: He ordered that all baby boys in Bethlehem
should be killed (Matthew 2:16). Herod missed the chance
to greet the Messiah because he was so caught up in
competing, comparing, and worrying.

In contrast, Luke introduces an elderly widow who
lived day and night in the Temple. She worshipped God
with her life. Since she was not concerned about herself,
she was among the first to meet the newborn Jesus.

We live in a self-oriented culture. When we are self-
absorbed, we cannot worship Jesus or see his path for our
lives. To have life, we must stop competing, comparing,
and worrying, and choose to live in joy and thankfulness.

Look past yourself to God!

Follow the Star

When they saw the star, they were filled with joy!
Matthew 2:10

The story of the wise men is familiar to many of us. Children learn the series of events that lead up to Jesus' birth with the shepherds, the angels, and the miraculous night in the Bethlehem stable. When the wise men found Jesus after their long journey, they experienced great joy. As they saw the star, they knew that God was alive, present, and at work in their lives. The wise men responded by seeking out the newborn King.

Jesus said, "Keep on asking, and you will receive what you ask for. Keep on seeking, and you will find. Keep on knocking, and the door will be opened to you. For everyone who asks, receives. Everyone who seeks, finds. And to everyone who knocks, the door will be opened" (Matthew 7:7-8). When we see God alive and at work in our world, we are filled with joy. God is real! As the wise men followed the star to Jesus, we, too, can seek and follow him.

God will become real in your life as you persist in seeking him.

God will reveal himself.

Free!

If the Son sets you free, you are truly free. John 8:36

Deep inside, we all have a longing to be distinctive. Our Creator shaped us in his own image and gave us certain abilities. When we tap into these strengths, we excel and our lives feel significant. If we faithfully follow God's path in using those strengths, we will satisfy our longing to be distinctive. We find out what we were created for.

Because of Jesus, we are set free to become the people we were meant to be. In life apart from God, our sins hold us back from the life we yearn for. In our culture, it is easier to let other people in our lives squeeze us into their mold than it is to discover our unique gifts. It is easier to be self-centered than to put these gifts at the service of others.

The expectations of others easily deter us from following God's lead and discovering what makes our hearts sing. Jesus came to free us from our faults and from the expectations of others. He makes it possible for us to follow him.

In the approaching New Year, allow yourself to laugh, live, love, and enjoy each day! Follow Jesus and be free!

Jesus frees us to be ourselves!

The Hands of Time

There the child grew up healthy and strong. He was filled with wisdom, and God's favor was on him.

Luke 2:40

Growth is a fact of life . . . for a time. In the flowers and trees of springtime, we discover God's gift of new life. In the caterpillars and butterflies of summer, we witness God's miraculous transformation into beauty. In fall, we watch the colors change as growth slows. In the winter, everything is still.

Jesus' life was marked by growth. He grew spiritually, physically, emotionally, and socially into the person who gave his life for ours!

Growth is still a choice for us as adults. If we choose to follow Christ, we must make this choice every day. We can learn to be open to having God's hands shape us into the women he intends for us to be.

As the hands of time move forward into the next moment, we must move forward in our spiritual growth. Begin each day with a prayer before your feet hit the floor. Make time to spend in silent connection with God. God will make your life into a more beautiful design than you could imagine! Live and grow today!

Allow time for growth.

Coloring Book

Choose today whom you will serve.   Joshua 24:15

As a girl, I loved to color. A box of crayons and a color-
ing book kept me busy for hours. It was fun to choose the
colors and bring a black-and-white picture to life.

Imagine your life in the upcoming year as a blank color-
ing book. You get to choose the picture to color, and you
get to choose the colors and where to apply them!

God loves us so much that he lets us decide what we
will do and who we will glorify with our lives. He hopes
that we will want to walk alongside him and choose his
perfect design for our lives, but he always gives us the
choice.

Reflect on your choices for the upcoming year. Will you
color a bright and sunny picture and invite love, peace, and
gentleness into your life? Or will you allow the dark colors
of criticism, comparison, and selfishness to overshadow the
brightness and joy your life could have?

Choose joy and serve God with your life. Choose
significance by serving others and growing daily into the
person you were made to be!

Our choices reveal our allegiance.

Powerful Promise

Jesus told him, "I am the way, the truth, and the life."

John 14:6

As we gaze at the next sheet on the calendar, we are peeking into next year. Think of the possibilities, the potential! The dreams you've held, the plans you've worked for, the vision that could be realized—all by this time next year! Standing on the threshold of a New Year is life changing. Lay your hopes and dreams in God's hands.

Jesus says that he is the way to God the Father. We can live confidently because Jesus walks with us. There is no reason to fear—only trust is needed.

Fear keeps us captive. To fly, we must break free of that fear. With God, all things are possible! Remember this powerful promise for the New Year: "Don't be afraid, for I am with you. Don't be discouraged, for I am your God. I will strengthen you and help you. I will hold you up with my victorious right hand" (Isaiah 41:10).

Allow God to hold you. Resist fear and live confidently each day as God's beloved child. Take courage and strength from Jesus, and allow him to make you a confident, loving, and courageous woman. May God give you a blessed New Year!

Happy New Year!

About the Author

Jennifer King writes from her personal faith journey and her experience of finding joy in simple, everyday life. Jennifer is a woman of many talents. She has been successful as an international model, a corporate engineer, a synchronized swimmer, and a classical violist.

Having chosen simplicity over her other successes, Jennifer loves the family-centered delight of being a full-time wife and the mother of three young boys. She has found significance in the most unexpected places, such as the miraculous beauty of a garden flower or the childish exuberance of a belly laugh. Her life has become full and rich, abundant and wholehearted. Jennifer finds joy in backyard gardening and floral photography, and her writing is another venue for Christ's message to shine through.

Jennifer and her husband, Brian, live with their sons in Ohio.

To experience nature's beauty through Jennifer's photography, visit www.jennifersgardens.com.

Do-able. Daily. Devotions.

START ANY DAY THE ONE YEAR WAY.

Do-able.
Every One Year book is designed for people who live busy, active lives. Just pick one up and start on today's date.

Daily.
Daily routine doesn't have to be drudgery. One Year devotionals help you form positive habits that connect you to what's most important.

Devotions.
Discover a natural rhythm for drawing near to God in an extremely personal way. One Year devotionals provide daily focus essential to your spiritual growth.

For Women

The One Year Devotions for Women on the Go

The One Year Devotions for Women

The One Year Devotions for Moms

The One Year Women of the Bible

The One Year Daily Grind

For Men

The One Year Devotions for Men on the Go

The One Year Devotions for Men

For Couples

The One Year Devotions for Couples

For Families

The One Year Family Devotions

For Teens

The One Year Devos for Teens

The One Year Devos for Sports Fans

For Bible Study

The One Year Life Lessons from the Bible

The One Year Praying through the Bible

The One Year through the Bible

For Personal Growth

The One Year Devotions for People of Purpose

The One Year Walk with God Devotional

The One Year at His Feet Devotional

The One Year Great Songs of Faith

The One Year on This Day

The One Year Life Verse Devotional

It's convenient and easy to grow with God the One Year way.

CP0162

Teach Truth.

MEET JESUS EVERY DAY THE ONE YEAR WAY.

For Kids

The One Year
Devotions for
Girls

The One Year
Devotions for
Boys

The One Year
Devotions for
Preschoolers

The One Year
Devotions for
Kids

The One Year
Make-It-Stick
Devotions

The One Year
Bible for Kids:
Challenge
Edition

The One Year
Children's Bible

The One Year
Book of Josh
McDowell's
Youth Devotions